Drowning in Doctrine

A Counselor Redefining Family
After Religious Trauma

Crystal W. Hamilton, LMHC

COPYRIGHT © Crystal W. Hamilton

www.redefinefam.com

Drowning in Doctrine: A Counselor Redefining Family After Religious Trauma

All rights reserved. This book is licensed for your enjoyment and remains the copyrighted property of the author. It may not be reproduced, copied, and/or distributed in any manner for commercial or non-commercial purposes without the author's express written permission, except in the case of brief quotations embodied in critical articles or reviews.

Published by: Redefine Family, LLC

ISBN
979-8-9986145-3-8 Hardback
979-8-9986145-0-7 Paperback
979-8-9986145-8-3 Ebook

Cover design by: Elena Dolevska
Edited by: Heather Ina

The stories in this book reflect the author's recollection of events. Some names, locations, and identifying characteristics have been changed to protect the privacy of those depicted. Some dialogue has been recreated from memory.

Dedication

To my husband, Scott, who has shown me what unconditional love truly is.

For my intuitive life coach, Natalie Alejandra Blanco, thank you for giving me the idea and courage to write this book. My work with Natalie has forever changed the trajectory of my life and connected me to my higher self.

This book is for those on the path to healing, whether beginning or already deep in the process. It is for those wrestling with faith, questioning their beliefs, or seeking a new way forward. May this book offer support, insight, and the courage to walk your own path with authenticity and strength.

Content Warning

This book contains discussions of sensitive topics, including but not limited to trauma, addiction, loss, violence, and systemic injustice. Some content may be triggering for readers who have experienced similar challenges.

Please take care of yourself while reading and remember that support is available 24/7 at 9-8-8.

If you live outside of the U.S., please reach out to a local mental health professional and/or crisis line to seek support.

Table of Contents

Introduction

Healing from religious trauma, a journey that demanded immense courage, has been challenging and transformative in my life. My upbringing in the Mormon faith, with its strict rules and heavy expectations, profoundly shaped my identity. When I couldn't meet those ideals, I was engulfed in shame.

My healing has been anything but a straight line. It's been a winding path through a fog full of unexpected twists and dead ends, with an occasional clearing. Therapy has been my compass guiding me through shadows I didn't even realize existed. The community I've found, other seekers and other survivors, remind me that I'm not walking this path alone, even when it feels that I am at times.

Slowly, I learned to loosen the grip of the rigid doctrines I was raised with and to see my self-worth as something that belongs to me. My self-worth is not something that's conditional on anyone else's approval. It's a strange and beautiful feeling to look in the mirror and feel a glimmer of acceptance. To feel my worth settle into my bones as something real, something permanent.

The healing journey isn't something that happens all at once. It's slow. Sometimes healing is excruciatingly slow. Each day, each small breakthrough is a reminder that it's worth it; that I am worth it. My story proves that we are all worth it, no matter what we have been through. That is, perhaps, the greatest gift of all.

Unknowingly Triggered

In 2013, my life felt that it was finally breaking open. After years of being bound by old patterns and clinging to relationships that stifled me, I was beginning to breathe on my own. For most of my life, I'd been deeply codependent with my identity entangled in the needs and expectations of others. I had finally uncoiled myself from associations that minimized me; I was determined to stand on my own two feet. I kept myself grounded, trying to steady myself and move forward with each shaky, exhilarating step. Earlier that summer, I had walked across a stage to receive my master's degree in counseling. It was a moment that felt surreal, as if I was watching someone else live out their dream.

It was easier to obsess over how far I had to go instead of focusing on how far I'd come. I was learning to celebrate the small victories, such as the first time I stood up for myself, or the moment I realized others' expectations no longer defined me. Slowly, I was taking pride in the person I was becoming.

Reflecting on my past, I could see the pain left me reeling, and it was ultimately pushing me toward a healing path. Without those struggles, I would not have found my way to counseling for personal growth and as a career. The year 2014 was the beginning of a journey that would reshape my entire life. Helping others by healing myself was my goal.

***

My second counseling session was winding down, and I couldn't deny a sense of relief. Observing my client's relationship with his mother echoed the struggles I'd watched my brother go through with our mother. At times, it was hard not to get triggered and pulled into my own past during his sessions. I fought the urge to tell him outright that he was not to blame for everything. Though I wanted to, I knew that putting my own ideas and personal experience onto him wasn't professional. This was not what he needed; therapy is not designed this way.

Instead, I held back, guiding him gently as he worked toward his own realizations with the dynamics between him and his mother. There's an art to letting clients find their own path to insight. When they're ready, they're ready.

As a counselor, I must ensure that I am taking care of my own healing to have patience for clients. We wrapped up the session with a few exercises he could practice independently; he could take small steps toward the clarity he sought. I jotted down notes on what we'd focus on next time while keeping one eye on the clock. There were just a few minutes to spare before my next appointment; a training session required to maintain my license.

Thirty-six hours every two years, including ethics, suicide prevention, and health equity courses, to keep my skills sharp and current, which is essential to my work. It is a solid reminder of the weight and responsibility I have to my clients.

I take immense pride in my accomplishments by supporting others in navigating their life choices. It is a role I once needed for myself. It was as if I could redefine my purpose through the support of helping others when they're lost. As I finished up and gathered my things, I felt a quiet excitement about stepping outside, if only for a few moments. The air was crisp and inviting, and I looked forward to stretching my legs and clearing my mind before diving back into more therapy and education.

The midday sun filtered through the blinds of my office as I grabbed my bag and slipped out just before the clock struck noon. Today I was solo, no colleagues, no familiar faces; just me, headed down the block to a local behavioral health hospital for training.

The routine of group seminars was comfortable, but I wanted something different this time. The trauma seminar caught my eye, offering a perfect blend of professional development and a free lunch. It was a great way to end the workday with free continuing education units and a meal. My keys jingled as I gathered them and dropped them in my bag. I said, "See you tomorrow" to a few coworkers before I left the building into the bright sunshine.

Although it was only the beginning of spring, the sun slightly warmed my skin, making the walk to the car even more enjoyable. It felt freeing, and the day's therapy sessions had melted away. I wouldn't need to repack that load until the following week. Just a short five-minute drive to the facility helped to refresh my mood.

Entering the hospital, the sterile scent of antiseptic hit me, causing my mood to digress a little. There was nothing like a shot of Vitamin D to activate the liveliness of my cells. Now, I could feel them quickly returning to hibernation once inside. I had been here before but today felt different. The training room buzzed with muted conversations; other therapists scanned handouts and sipped coffee. My mind was already churning through the afternoon's potential lessons about trauma. I found a seat near the back just in case my anxiety escalated, and I needed to escape without causing much disturbance. I was eager to learn something new. Three more hours of continuing education credit toward my license and my goal. I glanced at the clock; the smell of catered Panera Bread sandwiches wafted through the air as I made my way to the self-service line.

After I filled my plate with the essentials, I eased back into the chair where I had previously set my things. Once settled, I grabbed a fork and gave the entire room one more quick glance. My fork hovered over the salad, the lights dimmed slightly, and the first slide flickered onto the screen. Perfect timing. Just as I settled in, a woman dressed in cargo pants and a V-neck blouse strode to the front with purpose. She smiled briefly, her boots clicking sharply against the floor, and she introduced herself with a confident nod.

The PowerPoint began with a list of all the big traumas people endure, the effects, and how therapists can help clients address these issues in their lives. Information I was well-versed in allowed me to take more interest in the food I continued to devour. I took one huge bite and then another and continued to be mindful of the information being presented. Just as she was finishing up her talking point about rape, another slide flashed across the screen. The speaker paused to allow the audience to read it before she began.

"Little T's" or little traumas are the good things that didn't happen to us: not being seen or heard by caregivers, needs not being met, nutrients we didn't get. She held the clicker firmly as she continued to talk about many points on the slide. I read and listened intently as she listed a few.

"Things such as moving, having a mentally ill parent, leaving church, having sex when you felt you couldn't say no, chronic invalidation, and financial insecurity are all little T's," she intoned. I put my fork down and stared at the slide. The words "leaving church" glared back at me. "Oh, shit…" I mumbled quietly under my breath.

Suddenly, the meal was no longer appetizing. I stared at the extensive list of "Little T's" the entire time it was posted, as if the words would change the longer, I stared. LEAVING CHURCH was screaming at me in a way from which I could not divert. In that moment, I made the connection that leaving the Mormon Church was traumatic. I felt exposed. How could I have gone through graduate school and not recognize religious trauma?

This very simple reality I had dismissed, but leaving the Mormon Church was a trauma I had never verbalized as a trigger of posttraumatic stress disorder, or PTSD, as it's commonly called. I knew it was hard;

I didn't realize the magnitude of it. My adolescence began to flash before my eyes; I recalled instances in which I could connect religious indoctrinations to trauma responses. It made absolute sense because, when I left the church, I left a safety network and was absolutely alone. I lost my family, friends, and everything I knew. My whole world was turned upside down. I was alone to deal with a world filled with ways I could lose my way completely.

In my youth, when I felt that I had no support, I turned to drugs and alcohol to numb the pain. Being with others who I partied with gave me a false sense of belonging and connection. I had fragile connections that lasted until I'd black out. The drinking, partying, and even the part where I got sober, were all intertwined with the initial religious trauma. The connections were rooted, and there was no place I could turn to for safety. I knew then that the answers did not lie in the Mormon Church. That revelation was an important one, which came at the height of my panic attacks.

The realization I had trauma hit me like a ton of bricks. As I began to explore the concept further in my mind, the weight started to lift from my shoulders. Situations which I did not previously have the vocabulary for, I knew now was trauma. Another little "T" on the list was having sex when you felt that you could not say no. My mouth dropped open, and I was in awe. I had long forgotten his presence in my life, but it was vivid at that moment. A distant memory was now in the forefront of my mind.

These reflections felt as though I had been rear-ended and had whiplash. This was an 'aha' moment. It felt as if all the therapists in the room were staring at me knowingly. It was shock validation. I sat there frozen and sore from the revelations that had always been present in my life. Many different words and thoughts swirled in my head. I was dazed and speechless for the remainder of the seminar.

The walk back to my car was suffocating. I was dizzy, and my breathing was shallow. I wasn't going to make it back to my car without passing out. I had delved into all my family shit, the counseling I didn't receive as a teen, the stress that graduate school had caused, and now the stress of my daily work life. I was supposed to be helping others with their traumas, but I found myself falling apart. It was an out-of-body experience that caused me to pause once I was able to get my car unlocked. I hadn't even bothered to pull out my keys as I stood by the door, baffled by why I couldn't get inside.

After several moments of being drowned by all the thoughts swirling in my head, a moment of clarity allowed me to retrieve my keys and unlock the car with the push of a button. Slowly, I packed everything inside and situated myself to make the drive home. I gathered my thoughts and tried to compartmentalize them in a way that helped me see the positive side of this revelation.

At first, I felt good about connecting the dots to put my life in order. The further I drove; however, my positive energy flew out of the window of my car. Hope dissipated, and it was replaced with a looming feeling of grief. It was progressively becoming heavier to the point that I was having a hard time focusing on driving, and my eyesight blurred. My life story was playing out through a new chronological lens; it was through the lens of religious trauma I had made my choices.

For every year I spent in therapy and all subsequent years I served as a trained therapist to others, how could I just now acknowledge the depths of my own trauma? My spirit had been weighed down with something entirely different. I fell apart. Before I could react with logic, tears flowed down my face. I had to pull over to the side of the road. Had I been pixelated, I would have floated away to another realm, to reinvent myself and try again. Life is never easy, and because cathartic moments can be a shifting force that violently takes us from one state of being to the next, I struggled to gain my footing. I began to implode at the seams right in my car.

I found myself hyperventilating, unable to catch my breath, in a full-blown panic attack. I was using the coping skills that I was trained to use to try to calm the storm; it wasn't working. I was flooded with a multitude of emotions that had me dazed. I couldn't figure out which way was up or down. It was making me dizzy and sick to my stomach.

This was not the first time this had happened to me, so I recognized the signs immediately. I needed to hold on to reality and not dissociate. Validation of my feelings was the most important step to recovery. I kept telling myself to take all the time I needed to get my derailed mindset back on track so I could drive the rest of the way home. Standing on the side of the road, I was thinking how I had begun the day optimistically, and now I could feel waves of dreaded emotions swell and dissipate.

I tried to relax my violently shaking body and vibrating hands by walking to the back of the car so people driving by wouldn't be alarmed. To the passersby, it looked as though I was getting something out of my trunk. My heart felt as if it was beating its way out of my chest, slowly suffocating me and forcing me to shed even more tears. My mouth was dry, and I wanted to drink, but I could not control my tremors or breathing. I felt crazy standing there. I thought which route would be the easiest to get home, and I kept telling myself that I could drive the back roads as slowly as I wanted. I grabbed a cold drink to snap myself out of it but spilled it on my shirt because of my shaking hands. I wasn't as bothered by the wetness as I was by the thoughts circulating in my mind. I finally gathered enough will to drive. I made my way home in small increments, periodically stopping on the side of the road to let cars drive past me.

Family of Origin

I was the youngest of six, born in the sticky heat of New Orleans. I was a quiet child who learned early on to take up as little space as possible. My parents told me that, compared to my sisters, I was easy to love. I was the child who kept her head down and followed directions. I stepped lightly through childhood and was careful not to create any family turmoil compared to my older siblings. I did not want to be a burden.

My father was the last of six siblings himself, born to my grandmother when she was forty. Home for him was a remote Idaho farm, and his mother gave birth to him nearly ten years after his closest sibling. By the time he was old enough to help with chores, his older siblings were out of the house. His life consisted of early risings to wide open fields, milking cows, and tending crops. My mother grew up in a nearby city in a tense household where the clink of a bottle could make the walls shudder.

Her family was "Jack Mormon" in a town where Mormonism ran throughout the blood of the community. "Jack Mormon" was a scandalous whisper, labeling those who are members of The Church of Jesus Christ of Latter-Day Saints but don't follow the strict rules required to enter the temple.

My parents' paths crossed in the 1960s at Rick's College, a small Mormon school in Rexburg, Idaho. My father had returned from his two-year mission in the California-Arizona area, and my mother was attending nursing school. My mother told us that, when they were dating, she would put her large purse firmly between them in the car to keep his eager hands at bay. He would chuckle, nudging the purse playfully while she'd give him a sideways glance, eyebrows raised. They dated, fell in love, and dad proposed to my mother on Christmas Eve.

When my parents married in the Latter-Day Saints Temple, my maternal grandparents were deemed "unworthy" in the eyes of the church and not permitted to see their daughter exchange vows. My uncle told my mother that if she married in the temple, she would be out of the family. Against her family's wishes, my mother went forward with the wedding and sealed her nuptials in the temple. Her parents attended the reception afterwards. Since she was an active member of the church, she was the black sheep of her family. That rift between my mother and her parents never healed. My mother and father would speak of it in hushed tones, shaking their heads over old grievances that neither time nor forgiveness could mend.

My parents' marriage in the temple meant they adhered to the Mormon belief that they become an eternal family, sealed as partners for all time and eternity. The children you have, too, will be with you forever. All that is necessary is for you to behave appropriately on earth and you will go to Heaven to live in eternal bliss.

It's an all-or-nothing type of thinking; it's all good or all bad, with no room for shades of gray. I believe that thinking in absolutes leads to the Mormon community's propensity to be judgmental and critical of those who live in the shades of gray.

In recent years, the church began referring to itself as The Church of Jesus Christ of Latter-Day Saints (LDS) rather than "Mormon." LDS is the new name; members are no longer allowed to refer to themselves as Mormons. The teachings are the same: Obey the patriarch no matter what. He is the head of the family. The man obeys God, and the woman obeys the husband; therefore, women have no power. As a child, I did not fully understand the Mormon teachings. I did not understand the definition of "patriarch" until I reached age eighteen.

Before I'd taken my first breath, my parents agreed I would be raised in the faith, follow church teachings without question, and obey the patriarch of the family. A path of rigid rules and rituals had framed my life with early-morning scripture study, prayers, and stern warnings to "be in the world; not of the world." I learned at a young age that to be Mormon wasn't just a matter of faith; it was a matter of belonging. Falling out of step meant risking everything. The unspoken message was clear: if you weren't truly Mormon, you weren't truly one of us.

My childhood was mixed with innocent fun and deep grief that would take me a lifetime to untangle. I am still unable to separate my parents from the Mormon Church. To me, they are the same. Any conflicts I had at home were only magnified by the Morman beliefs my parents held. It seemed everything I loved and hated was intertwined so extensively that I couldn't separate one from the other.

Miracles woven into the fabric of my childhood began with an emphasis that the Mormon Church is true if a spiritual experience occurs. When I was four years old, my small body was burning with fever, and my cheeks were flushed and sticky with sweat. My parents wanted to take me to the hospital and decided to give me a patriarchal blessing before we left. My father removed the small tin container of blessed oil from his pants pocket, where he always kept it.

My mother and siblings sat next to me while I laid on the couch. My father poured the oil, put his hands on my forehead, and gave me a patriarchal blessing. He was halfway through the prayer when my fever broke. That mystical experience proved the Mormon Church was true. My parents called it a miracle, a sign that God was watching over me and I needed to stay true to the Mormon faith.

For years afterward, my parents would recall the miracle when I questioned the faith. They reminded me that I was healed because of our faith in the church. In their eyes, the fever had been a test. It was a moment that proved the strength of their faith; the path I was supposed to walk. The miracle was the reason I needed to stay in the church as I grew older. It was a memory that weighed on me, not as a miracle, but as an oppressive chain which bound me to a church and faith I had not chosen for myself.

In the Mormon community, there were always people around. There was always someone I could talk to and feel support from. Smoking and drinking were banned. Not even cola or tea was allowed in our house. Those substances would affect the natural, divine chemistry of the brain and, therefore, were forbidden. I had a creative outlet at church by participating in pageants, talent shows and acting in skits. I cherish those fun memories.

On the other hand, when I was four years old, my parents drove off with my older siblings and left me at the church. They simply forgot about me. I was terrified at that moment, and the event sealed my spirit with feelings of abandonment. As I grew older, I drifted into complacency and let life happen to me instead of reaching for what I needed. It was as if that moment taught me, without words, that I didn't deserve to take up space. Though I couldn't make sense of the pain I carried, it remained with me, woven into my choices and tied to the quiet ways I learned to punish myself for not being a good Mormon girl.

As kids, my brother and I were inseparable. We were bound by endless dares and the thrill of testing boundaries. He was only a year older; just enough to make him the leader of our little two-person gang. He was constantly dreaming up new ways to get us in trouble.

One afternoon, as my dad rummaged through the refrigerator, my brother leaned close, his eyes gleaming with mischief, and said, "I dare you to bite Dad's butt." He was barely able to contain his laughter as he whispered. I stared at him, mouth open in shock, feeling my face heat up as I glanced at our dad, still oblivious and bent over with his head buried in leftovers.

"No way," I whispered back, half-laughing, half-terrified. But then my brother grinned and said, "If you do it, I'll do it too."

That was all it took. My heart pounded in my chest, each beat daring me to move forward. I felt a wild, nervous energy buzzing through me. It was the kind you get when you're about to do something you know is a bad idea. I crept closer; my brother nudged me forward with a barely concealed snicker. I had just a second to steady myself. My pulse was racing; my body was on edge, and then I lunged forward, sinking my teeth into the fabric of my dad's pants.

My dad instantly jerked upright and yelled in surprise as he spun around. His face displayed a mix of shock and bewilderment. My brother burst into laughter behind me and doubled over as I tried to back away, wide-eyed, with cheeks burning.

"Who did that?!" my dad sputtered, still trying to process what had just happened. I stammered, trying to point at my brother, but he was already on the floor, laughing too hard to breathe. Needless to say, he never got his turn; the dare was over. The look on my dad's face was worth it.

Another afternoon, my brother Sean and I found a pair of our dad's underwear in the laundry pile. Mormons do not wear regular underwear bought from the store; they wear garments that symbolize the covenants taken in the temple. My dad's garments were a perfect prop for a prank. Without a second thought, we each claimed a leg hole, Sean on one side, me on the other, and started waddling around the house. The oversized waistband pulled us together as we stumbled and laughed. We shuffled down the hallway, barely able to keep our balance, trying not to collapse as we called out to the rest of the family, our voices bubbling with laughter.

"Look at us! We're Dad!" We shouted, wobbling side to side like some strange, two-headed creature. The sight of us, two little kids tangled up in dad's garments, sent our siblings into fits of laughter. Even our dad, when he caught sight of us, just shook his head, chuckling as he watched us parade around with the pride of clowns.

Moments like these stitched Sean and me together in a way that was different from my connection with my sisters, who were much older and often busy with other things. With Sean, it was simple. We shared jokes, silly dares, and laughter that echoed through the house. Those events bound us in the same way as that oversized waistband in dad's garments and pulled us together in ties that would last a lifetime.

My childhood was filled with fond memories about family camping trips with my dad teaching us how to camp and fish. I can still smell the damp earth, pine needles, and the smoky scent of campfire clinging to my clothes as the sun dipped below the trees. My dad knelt beside me with steady hands as he showed me how to drive the stakes into the ground, where each thud of the mallet made my small arms ache. "Like this," he said, his voice warm and patient. He guided my hands as I fumbled with the tent poles. Together, we'd pull the canvas tight, stepping back to admire our crooked little shelter with a shared grin of accomplishment.

Later, Dad would wrap potatoes, carrots, and chunks of meat in tin foil and let me crimp the edges before we buried them in the coals. The sizzle and crackle filled the silence of the forest. My stomach rumbled with anticipation as we waited and swapped fishing stories by the fire. When he handed me a fishing pole the next morning, his big hand covering mine as he taught me to cast, I heard the cool lake splashing against my boot and felt the thrill of the line pulling taut. Each lesson, wrapped in laughter with the smell of campfire smoke, was like a secret he passed down to me. Those memories glowed warmly in my mind years later.

There were also dark days in my family that I did not fully understand. I was young when the entire family set out for a long drive to Idaho for the annual family reunion. My eldest siblings, Lindsey and Sarah, ages fourteen and sixteen respectively, sat in the back seat, silent and tense. It was as if they knew something the rest of us didn't. The trip was long and sticky, with hot wind blowing through the car windows, the ripped ceiling hanging down in bubbles and us, the youngest three, with our feet hanging out of the back window of our brown station wagon.

Lindsey came out to my parents as gay; she was considered an embarrassment, and my parents took her to live with our maternal grandmother in Idaho. Sarah refused to leave her sister behind and was left to live with our paternal grandmother. Just like that, they were gone from us. For the next five years, Lindsey lived in Idaho.

We piled back into the car, minus two, and drove back to New Orleans. My heart was confused, but I was too scared to question what happened. As the scenery shrunk in the rearview mirror, I didn't understand it then, but I felt the shift in the air. Another warning that drifted through the years was settling like dust on everything I did: don't step out of line, or you'll get left behind, too.

My dad's mother had a stroke; Sarah moved with the cousins who also took care of our grandmother. Two years later, Sarah returned to New Orleans. She revealed to my parents how our cousin, who was married in the temple and had young children, had molested her. Both our parents were open about what had happened, which was strange because our family was never open about anything. I could hear only bits and pieces of their conversations.

I was eight years old and couldn't understand the discussion. Sarah showered five times a day and kept the living room blinds shut. She refused to sleep in her bedroom alone. I was by her side constantly; she took me to the store or Toddle House every day because she didn't want to be alone. I could not understand why. When we walked down the street together, she would scold me if I smiled at strangers: "Don't talk to anybody, not even to say hello."

No police were involved, but our parents told the perpetrator's bishop about the molestation. To cope with the sexual assault, my parents told my sister to talk to their bishop in New Orleans. This bishop blamed my sister for the molestation. Sarah ran out of the church that day and didn't come home for days. Another message I learned in childhood was that I was "less than" because I was female, and the man would always have authority over me, no matter what. What did all this mean? I was unsure, but at that young age, I took it to mean that this was going to be my way of life. If I followed Mormon rules, I belonged. If I didn't, then I would be banished just as my sisters had been.

We moved into our first two-story house when we returned from Idaho. I sat cross-legged on the carpet in the living room with my sister, half-listening to the muffled shouts coming from down the hall. My two older sisters, Sarah and Lindsey, were at it again, their voices raised in the familiar rhythm of argument, their words tangled in frustration. My mother appeared in the doorway, her expression calm and thoughtful, as if this were no more than a simple math problem to be solved.

Mother waited until the shouting died down and

called them into the kitchen. My sisters shuffled in, eyes red and arms crossed. I expected Mom to suggest separate rooms. After all, wasn't that the obvious solution when two people couldn't stand each other? She turned instead to the oldest, her voice measured and strangely philosophical. "Well, Lindsey," she said, tilting her head thoughtfully, "you'll be going to college soon. You'll have roommates there, and after that, you'll get married. So really, this is your last chance to live on your own." She paused as if savoring her logic, and then added, "You should have your own room now, while you still can."

I stared at my mother, waiting to hear a punchline that never came. It felt surreal. My brother lost his room and, as a result, had to sleep on a mattress where the wet bar would have been, but as Mormons, we used it as a closet. Lindsey's and my brother's life was planned with the same certainty she might use to rearrange the furniture. Where other parents may have enforced a break in warring sisters' company, my mom framed it as a gift; it was a logical step toward adulthood. I glanced at Sarah, whose expression had shifted from defiance to confusion. A hint of relief tugged at the corner of her mouth. The solution was so typical of my mother. It was unusual yet absolute and packaged with a tidy sense of practicality.

The house I grew up in was chaotic, dirty and, unkept. There was usually a carton of milk left sitting on the counter to spoil. I'd visit my friends' houses and walk through an immediate wave of order and calm; it was as if I was stepping into a magazine spread. Their moms would greet me with a warm smile while folding laundry or stirring food in a pot on the stove. Their floors were spotless, and neatly labeled containers lined pantry shelves. One friend's home had rows of perfectly stacked and labeled clear plastic bins of cereal; a small army of breakfast choices just waiting to be poured. Clothes vanished from bedroom floors and reappeared clean and folded on beds as if by magic.

Our house was nothing like that. It looked perfectly respectable from the outside with a freshly mowed lawn, but once you stepped through the front door, you could see it was clearly chaotic. Shoes and papers lay scattered across the entryway. Bills were tucked in the side of room switches to remind my mother to pay them and clutter reigned on every available surface. The air always seemed a little stale, tinged with a faint smell of burnt microwave popcorn, and the floor was sticky from soda spills that hadn't been mopped for days.

The living room, the room on the right when you walked into our home, was the only clean room. We were not allowed in that room unless there were guests. Every other room in the house looked like that one junk drawer everyone has in their kitchen. I'd learned to do my own laundry by the time I was eight. I was usually on my own at our house, navigating the mess and making do, longing for a sense of stability and ease that other kids seemed to take for granted.

Despite not having achieved perfection, I did feel that I knew exactly who I was and where I was going. I remember standing barefoot on the cold tile floor in a white baptismal gown. The room was quiet save for the soft murmur of family and friends who had gathered to watch. Their faces were expectant and proud. At just eight years old, I barely understood the weight of it all, but I felt it. A quiet pressure settled over me as I stepped into the warm water. When my father lowered me under, the world went muffled and still as if it was holding its breath. As I rose, blinking against the light, I saw my mother wiping her eyes. Her smile was soft and resolute.

Feeling the Pressure

My family went to Mississippi on a camping trip. The adults had cabins, and the kids slept in tents outside. The rain hammered down and turned our tent walls into a drumming chorus that drowned out the night sounds. I could see the faint glow of the cabin lights through the trees, where my parents were warm and dry, but here, as Sean and I huddled in our sleeping bag, the dampness crept in. While my brother and I slept, one by one, the older kids dashed to the cabin and left us behind. I woke up to a chill seeping through my clothes and realized we were lying in an inch of water. I glanced at Sean, his face pale and wide-eyed in the dark. We just stared, each waiting for the other to figure out what to do. That was what every day felt like in our home; he and I were left to fend for ourselves.

Fending for myself was the theme of my childhood. I was given tools that didn't necessarily connect with the views of the rest of world outside our community, and I was forced to fend for myself whether I was inside or outside the protection of my family. It was baffling to make sense of my life without outside influences, but with them, I was inundated and felt continuous pressure to be someone who didn't even resemble who I felt I was.

Except for my sister Sarah, our family moved from New Orleans to Houston, Texas, when I was in fifth grade. Sarah was in a relationship with a man around our father's age, and she chose to stay in New Orleans with him. It was a difficult decision for all of us to accept, but it was one she felt compelled to make.

The complexities of my childhood experiences began to unfold in a clearer light during a family reunion. My aunt was discussing my eldest sister, Lyndsey, and her girlfriend. I had known for quite some time that she was gay; Lyndsey had been in a committed relationship with a woman for many years. It made me question the true nature of our family's acceptance and values. The more I thought about it, the more I realized my questions weren't just about family; they touched on the faith I had leaned on. Guilt became my constant companion, with shame not far behind.

After church, I could hear my parents gossiping in the kitchen about church members, and then the discussion turned to my two older sisters. I heard my father's voice drop to a low, angry mutter. I knew that tone. It was sharp as a blade and reserved for moments when he thought no one was listening. The way my father spoke about my sisters, as if they were burdens or disappointments, sucked the air out of the room. Every syllable of every word felt like a punch that hit me deeper, because these were my sisters.

I was frozen there. My fingers curled into fists at my sides; my heart pounded with a mixture of shame and helplessness. I stayed hidden, silent, as his words hung in the air like poison. I was too afraid to breathe. A familiar weight settled over me. It was the same feeling I'd carried for years. It was the sense that by staying quiet, I was complicit, and yet, I did what I always did. I swallowed my anger, smoothed my face into a neutral mask, and played the role in which I'd been cast. I was the quiet daughter. The obedient one. I was the one who didn't rock the boat. When I finally stepped into the room, I plastered on a smile and pretended I hadn't heard a thing as my insides churned with resentment.

Faith felt hollow, an echo that meant pretending was good and truth was bad. I went through the motions, clinging to routine. At the age of twelve, I poured myself into my Gospel in Action record, setting goals and ticking them off one by one, as I was told. I still believed doing so would somehow deliver me from my own personal hell. It was the one thing I could still control. It was the one thing that made me feel that I was accomplishing something good.

Each day was a checklist of reading the scriptures,

personal prayer, and journaling. My mother's signature scrawled approval, and my teacher verified planned community activities. I memorized the Articles of Faith, each one feeling heavier than the last.

Church leaders encouraged us to keep a journal, and I filled page after page. The literature was either Mormon Church approved or the product of an LDS writer.

We had weekly family scripture study, daily family prayers, and attended three hours of church on Sundays. As an adolescent, in Young Women's we recited the Motto with reverence:

> *We are daughters of our Heavenly Father*
> *who loves us, and we love him.*
> *We will stand as witnesses, of God at all times*
> *and in all things, and in all places…*
> *as we strive to live the Young Women Values,*
> *which are Faith, Divine Nature, Individual*
> *Worth, Knowledge, Choice and Accountability,*
> *Good Works, and Integrity.*
>
> *We believe as we come to accept and act upon*
> *these values, we will be prepared to make and*
> *keep sacred covenants, receive the ordinances of*
> *the temple, and enjoy the blessings of exaltation.*

It was a carefully curated life of faith, but deep down,

I knew I was not being authentic. Walking on eggshells had worn me down, leaving only resentment for having ever believed in more.

My brother and I hardly spoke as we entered our pre-teen years. The closeness we once enjoyed had long dissipated; it was another lifetime. He had started drinking, using drugs, and getting into trouble at school. His anger filled every corner of the house and consumed my parents, my sister, and me—everyone who still lived in the house. The sudden clatter of a TV remote smashing against the wall or the gleam of a knife thrown from the kitchen to the den left me paralyzed. Each time, I'd catch myself tensing, my feet unconsciously moving to avoid the sharp words and glances, as if I could somehow dodge the storm.

I felt like an outsider drifting through crowded junior high school hallways. When my brother got into trouble at our school, my mother took him to the school where she taught. My faith had set me apart. Whispers and sideways glances followed me. Some kids told me that Mormons were a cult, and their parents forbade them to talk to me. I could spend the night at one friend's house, but they were not allowed to even visit my house. I hadn't begun to question my beliefs, yet it had begun to cost me friendships. I learned not to tell school friends that I was Mormon.

In seventh grade, I chose to attend the same

school as my brother, where my mother was a teacher. I transferred from a white middle-class neighborhood obsessed with designer clothes to the south side of Houston, where my face was one of few that didn't blend in. I realized what it meant to be in the minority. It was a constant sense of being on display.

With multiple moves to cities and states, I often lost touch with friends. Kerry was my one constant friend from elementary school. Her letters were a lifeline; she filled their pages with our secret jokes and dreams.

***

In my ninth-grade year, I met Randy while visiting a friend in Louisiana. He and I racked up huge long-distance phone bills talking to each other. It was 1994, and we often made mixtapes of songs we heard on the radio. The songs filled my teenage angst. Randy and I chose "Patience" by Guns N' Roses to be "our" song. I played our song on my mixed tape for months while thinking about Randy:

Shed a tear 'cause I'm missing you
I'm still alright to smile
Girl, I think about you every day now
Was a time when I wasn't sure

33

But you set my mind at ease
There is no doubt you're in my heart now
Said woman, take it slow,
it will work itself out fine
All we need is just a little patience

Randy was the first boy who made my pulse race. He was a distraction. I threw myself into him with a desperation I didn't want to admit. Focusing on him felt easier than facing the voids in my family, where the silent tension seeped through every dinner and every forced smile. Being with Randy was like catching my breath. It was a brief escape from the weight of trying to hold my silence in a family that was frayed.

By age fifteen, my brother had been to jail, to his first rehab, and he had been expelled from school. I was getting fed up with having to walk on eggshells to not upset him.

One day my sister and I were talking shit about him after he had stolen my mom's car and wrecked it in a ditch. He walked over to me, called me a slut, and proceeded to climb the stairs, as if what he had said meant nothing. I ran after him because I wasn't going to let him talk to me that way. His response was to kick me in the face, and I tumbled down the stairs. I stayed home from school the next day. I was full of despair and depression set in. When I stayed home the second day, my mother looked me in the eye and said, "Get over it." I went back to school on the third day.

My parents were inconsistent in how they showed their love and concern for me. I think they were more concerned about protecting the only son in the home rather than protecting their daughters. I feared for my safety every day and wondered whether my belongings would be stolen.

My sister and I had locks on our bedroom door, and a bracket ensured my brother could not get into our room and take our belongings. We couldn't leave our purses and other valuables on the kitchen table because they could be pawned for money to buy drugs. I became good at hiding things, including my true self.

When I was with my Mormon friends, I had to act a certain way. I wore an alternate mask wherever I was. I could not really be my authentic self with church friends and family, but with my boyfriend, I was different.

I held several leadership positions at church that helped me learn to live with values and principles. I participated in team activities and have great memories of playing volleyball, basketball, and attending girls' camp. Rigid gender roles were ingrained into the youth. While the girls were taught to be codependent and obey their husbands, the boys were playing basketball. The girls made crafts, cooked, baked, and compiled a list of ideal characteristics their future husband needed to have. The status quo in the Mormon Church was, and still is, sexism. Even my father routinely made sexist jokes. "Everything went downhill after women got the right to vote; Eve ate the apple first," he would say.

Mormons believe that after death, spirits wait in another plane until they are accepted into the Celestial Kingdom, which is the highest of the three-tiered Heaven planes. To meet one of the Covenants and get to the top of Heaven, Mormons must baptize non-members by proxy. The Spirits will choose whether to accept the baptism. Visits to the temple must be approved by the bishop. Baptisms for the Dead and Confirmations for the Dead may occur if the bishop deems one worthy of entering the temple.

It's an exciting time to go to the temple in youth group. Since the closest temple was in Dallas, Texas, it was an all-day event. Sometimes the activity required the youth to stay the night.

The first trip I was old enough to take, I couldn't because of my menstrual cycle. A youth group leader told me, "You can't go in there because you'll taint the water." That is true if a girl is wearing a pad, but being the pre-teen little girl I was, I took it to mean that being a female was dirty. Hearing the statement made me think something was wrong with me. I thought there must be something wrong with my body and femininity.

My brother was thirteen years old and went on the Temple trip. He came back that day and said, "You got your period. That's why you didn't go." Oh, the joy of having an older brother! When my brother saw a sanitary pad or tampon commercial, he would say, "That's what Crystal needs." What resonated with me was that being a woman is unclean. After all, I couldn't perform baptisms because of my menstrual cycle. I unknowingly held on to resentment about that until adulthood.

By the time I was fourteen years old, Sunday school lessons had become an endless loop of how to have a temple marriage, which was the only proper ending for a Mormon girl. Lessons turned into exercises. Sunday school leaders handed us worksheets filled with questions about "the ideal man" and encouraged us to make a list of desired traits. Each activity circled back to the same point, which was marriage. Sunday lessons would often include a picture of a girl in front of the temple, her veil flowing and framing her like a promise. The message was unmistakable and woven into every lecture and lesson: marriage was the goal.

Church was at the center of all my activities. I couldn't escape participation. One day before the sacrament meeting began, I was sitting in the pew talking to my friends. I wore a wrap-around skirt, which had unraveled, exposing my leg. My friend's father stared at my legs the entire time I re-wrapped the skirt. It made me uncomfortable. I remember thinking that my dad would have turned his head. This man did not; this man, who had been married in the temple and was father to four daughters, stared at me seductively. The day he was teaching Sunday School; I told my mom I didn't want to go to his class. My mom said I could go to class with her.

In my mom's class, I heard a woman say some things that were not so nice about women who chose to work. The woman said, "I'm not talking about women who must work because their husbands don't make enough money to support the family. I'm talking to the women who choose to work because they don't want to stay home with their children." She bad-mouthed women who wanted to have careers of their own. I turned, with a questioning look, to my mother, who has had a job since I was born, and she told me to just ignore her.

There were plenty of contradictions about the role of Mormon women. These messages affected my self-esteem and decision-making abilities. Looking back on that day, I can definitely say I was "frozen" and not sure what to do with myself. Should I fight, flight, or freeze? How could I ignore the messages I received from this ideology my entire life?

When I was younger, I was attracted to girls and

to boys. When my oldest sister was left in Idaho because she was a gay teenager, I knew that same-sex feelings were not tolerated in my family or my church. My sister proved that this type of relationship was something our family did not accept. I was attracted to this girl during my freshman year of high school. We fooled around a bit, and I hid this from my parents, but somehow they knew. They gave me the option of speaking to the bishop, but they didn't mandate it because they remembered my older sister had run away from home after talking to the bishop. They were worried I was gay, so they decided to let me start dating at the age of fourteen. Typically, Mormon girls do not date until they reach age sixteen.

Dating boys was the goal, but I don't think my parents thought I was having sex. As soon as they allowed me to date, things progressed quickly. I met a guy named Aaron in band class, and we began dating during the second half of my freshman year. He was a high school junior, seventeen years old, and drove a truck. I was trying my best to be a good little Mormon girl, but the lure of meeting my first love got the best of me.

First Date - February 6, 1994 - Journal Writing:

Call me a rebel or what- yesterday I went on date with Aaron. He picked me up and I ran out of the house. Then my dad called me back and asked where I was going and

with who. Of course I lied. I told him we were going out
with lots of people. Aaron and I went to Chili's. He paid
for everything. We saw the movie "Philadelphia." I liked
it a lot, but it was depressing, and Aaron didn't like it.
We were in front of my house, and when I said I'd better
go, and he said, "Well what about a kiss?" So, I leaned
over and gave him a French kiss, but I think I caught
him off guard. I felt his braces. This was his first kiss ever,
and our first kiss was awkward.

Freshman year I started smoking cigarettes to stay thin, kissing boys and girls and drinking Zima at the park. I had begun taking birth control pills to regulate my menstrual cycle and didn't have to hide them. We lived in a new housing development, and there were an ample number of abandoned houses and cul-de-sacs where Aaron and I could park and make out. Every day, I wore a Choose the Right ring and a Young Women's medallion. Every day, I took off my Mormon jewelry and gingerly placed it on the truck dashboard while we made out at our favorite place, Distant Rock. After the police caught us making out in the truck several times, Aaron and I began sneaking upstairs to his bedroom while his parents were sleeping.

We had sex the first time on his bedroom floor during the summer before my sophomore year. I cried afterwards. I knew I had sinned, was no longer pure for my husband, and not worthy for marriage in the temple. My dad continually asked me if I was having sex, and I continually denied that I was. My dad said, "You got birth control pills for one reason, but now you're taking them for another reason."

" Nope" was always my reply when he asked.

Two of my brother's friends moved into our home during my sophomore year. One night, my boyfriend Aaron brought me home in his big, brown, beat-up truck after my parents were asleep. My brother and his friends sat on the curb in front of the house smoking. When we pulled up, they stood and yelled at us while my brother waved a bat. I told Aaron to stay in the truck and I jumped out. I was paralyzed with fear that the situation would escalate to the point that someone would call the police. It didn't, but it bothered me that my parents condoned him having friends living in our home doing drugs.

My parents allowed my brother's abusive behavior in our home, but they had no problem sending their two eldest daughters to live 1,500 miles away when they disobeyed them or church rules. Meanwhile, my brother had the lay of the land. My parents tolerated it when he called me a slut or threatened to hit my boyfriend. They simply told me to keep my mouth shut and "keep the peace."

In many ways, I was like the other schoolgirls my age

41

who were having sex with their boyfriends after attending school dances or band banquets. At the same time, I was going to Seminary Meetings before school and church on Wednesday nights and on Sunday mornings to receive explicit instructions on how to be the ideal Mormon wife.

At the end of tenth grade, I was so engulfed with shame, I admitted to my bishop that I was having sex. I don't remember how the conversation went, but I do remember not feeling relieved after confessing my sins. The bishop recommended I read a book. Months before, I took it upon myself to stop taking sacrament.

I broke up with Aaron when I turned sixteen. I had my driver's license, and I had a few close friends. We drank Zima when we could get a friend's brother to buy them for us. My friends had gotten their first jobs, and we frequently went to their twenty-three-year-old boss' apartment to party. We drank and had sex, which deeply worsened my shame. One night when we were drinking, I met Hayden, who had come by to drink with his coworkers. He gave me his pager number, and we later started dating. Hayden was a nineteen-year-old, shy virgin that I entangled in my shameful spiral. I pursued him and initiated sex since he hadn't experienced it before.

Everyone had an opinion about how I presented

myself and what I should be doing with my life. I wasn't quite sure what I wanted, but I knew that where I was wasn't my ideal. My brother would often call me a slut for wearing something as simple as a halter top. I could not respond to his insults because, if I did, my mom would yell at me. I thought I was bad because I got a second ear piercing. I had stopped taking sacrament because I felt so ashamed. Besides, you can't take sacrament if you are unworthy.

My dad said to me one day, "You know, you need to start taking sacrament." Unlike the Catholic Church, where you walk up to the altar to receive it, in the Mormon Church, boys go row by row, handing a tray to the person at the end of each pew. Each person passes the tray to the next person after taking the bread and water, so people know when you don't take sacrament. It was easy for my parents to see me pass the sacrament. I remember my mom let out a nervous laugh when she saw me pass the sacrament. It wasn't that she thought it was funny; she was appalled. Her nervous laugh was her way of dealing with my new reality.

My sister's former high school boyfriend, Justin, came to live with us after attempting suicide. At the time, I believe my brother was out of the house, had completed rehab, was released from jail, and living on the street, though I really don't remember. Justin was enrolled at Brigham Young University, and he had attempted suicide because he was gay. Justin no longer wanted to live with his parents, so my parents allowed him to live with us. He and I sat together with my family at church each Sunday, not taking sacrament for months. I never took sacrament again.

Foreseen Consequences

In our family, the rules for girls were clear-cut. There were no gray areas; it was perfection or nothing. The rules for my brother? That was a different story. While we walked a tightrope, he seemed to have free reign to push boundaries. The girls were bending over backwards to accommodate him. He'd been kicked out of more than one school, each expulsion only adding to his legend. He continued to take drugs, have sex, and physically assault his girlfriends. Our house was his kingdom, and each of us cowered to his temper and whims. I learned to keep quiet, smooth over the chaos he left in his wake, and I wore my compliance like a badge. It was my role and my silent sacrifice.

My brother was a storm no one could control, and the rest of us scrambled to pick up the pieces he left behind. Each misstep, each burst of chaos, was swept under the rug and carefully hidden. Our family was bound together by secrets whispered in hallways and omissions that spread like roots beneath the surface. It felt like a web tightening around me; it was a mesh of lies and half-truths that made breathing feel impossible. I could feel it slowly suffocating something inside me; it was a heaviness that left me hollow and longing to escape a life that didn't feel like mine.

Meanwhile, my brother continued his trail of destruction, going in and out of drug rehab. At fifteen, he had gotten a twelve-year-old girl pregnant. My parents said they prayed about it, and the Lord said it would be okay. My parents seemed determined to do whatever it took to protect him.

Part of my brother's rehabilitation after interacting with the courts included individual and family counseling. I told the counselors about everything that was happening at home with my brother. In one session, we talked about the incident where my brother kicked me down the stairs. Child Protective Services came to the school and pulled me out of class to talk about the incident. I told the caseworker that it was my brother who kicked me, not my parents. Sibling violence was always dismissed in my home, as if it wasn't anything to worry about.

The attention I received from guys was the only thing that offset the fear and isolation I felt. The attention from boys boosted my self-esteem and simultaneously tore me apart. The pressure to be perfect all the time was damaging to my spirit. My opinion was that the Mormon religion preyed on the inability of children to think critically. The Mormon Church brainwashes you into believing the hypocrisy and revering the stagnant growth of women.

I feel sad for my young teenage self that endured feelings of shame from a religion that told me I was a sinner. I slipped through the days like a ghost, quiet and unnoticed, careful not to stir up a ruckus at home. My role was that of the "lost child." I was the one who didn't cause trouble. I'd sit through church with my Mormon necklace resting neatly on my collarbone and nod "Yes" to every teaching. Later, I'd unclasp the necklace in the presence of my boyfriend and tuck it away as if shedding a part of my skin. The weight inside me grew heavier; a dark fog crept into every corner of my mind. Smiling felt impossible. It was as though I was holding a heavy mask in front of my face that I could barely lift. I was sinking, and no one noticed my disappearance.

I celebrated, just as any sixteen-year-old Mormon girl would, with wholesome games, apple bobbing, and hitting a piñata. Most of my guests were Mormon; we played games and enjoyed ourselves in a very innocent manner. Although, on a daily basis, I straddled the fence between partying, drinking, doing drugs, and maintaining my image as a good Mormon girl.

My mother blamed the boys and thought they were the reason I seemed out of balance, but the truth was my emotions had always felt that they were a rolling tide, unpredictable and constantly shifting beneath the surface. I had mostly mastered the art of holding it together, but my focus was slipping now. Good grades that had once been my anchor began to drift, though they still looked solid compared to my siblings'.

It felt that life was spinning out of control faster than I could keep up. Most days, I'd come home, throw myself across my bed, and the tears soaked my pillow by nightfall. I felt numb, unmotivated, as though I'd lost my grip on everything that once mattered.

One night, I decided I'd fake it, plaster on a smile, and pretend to be happy. Tomorrow, I told myself, would be a fresh start. My brother had graduated from rehab, was sober again, and had returned to school and church. Things were looking up for him. Now, it was my turn to fall further from grace.

My mom watched from a distance, unsure how to reach me, while I clung to the only answer I'd been taught: repentance. Just the thought that I needed cleansing only sank me deeper into the shadows, and a spiral of guilt and shame that pulled me further under began. Depression hit me hard, and my mother took me to the doctor, who gave me a prescription for Zoloft. I did not, however, receive individual counseling.

My brother was the "scapegoat" and center of our family's chaos, and I was the "lost child" sunk into a deep depression with the weight of it anchoring me to the couch. Mornings blurred into afternoons as I stared blankly at the walls, unable to summon the energy to go to school. One afternoon, I sat in the living room with my mom, and her voice broke through the haze.

"Do you want to drop out?" she asked. The question hung in the air like a quiet agreement. In my world, leaving school didn't seem like a failure; it felt like an escape. My purpose as a Mormon woman was clear: get married and start a family. Amid my turmoil, I made the decision. I dropped out of school one month into my junior year.

Shame wrapped around me like a heavy cloak, suffocating and oppressive. I was my own worst critic. I replayed every misstep and perceived flaw in my mind and chipped away at any shred of confidence I had left. The fear of sharing my struggles loomed large like a dark cloud that stifled my voice. I held back constantly, hesitant to let anyone see the turmoil brewing beneath my withdrawn demeanor. Conversations felt like tightrope walks. I worried I would be judged or misunderstood if I revealed too much; I kept everything bottled up. I was a silent prisoner to my own emotions, and I felt increasingly isolated as I guarded the fragile secret of my truth.

After taking some time off, rediscovering excitement while hanging out with Hayden, I went back to school. I re-enrolled in an alternative school, Windfern High, during the spring semester. Windfern had a college atmosphere with a laid-back vibe and autonomy. I could walk across the street to smoke cigarettes, then go back to class. This was a refuge from the chaos of my family and the shame that clung to me. I was still conflicted, had started taking antidepressants, and tried to attend church as the good girl.

On the other hand, Hayden was magnetic, and I felt alive around him. Especially at that party where I flirted shamelessly and leaned into the reckless energy of youth. His Mustang gleamed under the moonlight, reveling in its promise of freedom. He lived next door to Windfern in his parents' house, and I often skipped classes to go there.

One night, Hayden and I went to his house to make out after attending a party. We quickly became annoyed that my parents were calling his pager while we were fooling around. My heart raced, and excitement coursed through my veins as he slowly drove me home. My parents' frantic calls to his pager were a distant echo, and we laughed as we tried to remain detached. A police car stood guard outside, and suddenly, the thrill of the night evaporated. It was replaced by a rush of panic as reality crashed around us.

Hayden approached my house slowly. There was no way to sneak up to a house at one a.m. if you were riding in a car with a V8 engine. My dad walked out of the door, waved his arm for us to come inside, and yelled, "You'd better come in!"

We walked into the living room, and two police officers stood with my parents. "If you're having sex, we're gonna take you down to do a rape kit and put him in jail," my dad exclaimed.

I sat on the couch next to my mother while the officers took Hayden outside to question him. I wasn't sure how to feel, but one thought I had was that the entire scene was unwarranted. The police felt my parents were blowing things out of proportion, but they had to do their job. There was some back and forth, but mostly there was my refusal to speak. I shut down.

When the cops left, my mother spoke her mind and said, "You are such a slut." It stung. Her fifteen-year-old son had impregnated a twelve-year-old, but I was a sixteen year-old slut. As I ran upstairs, I caught a glimpse of my sister running to her bedroom. She had been sitting at the top of the stairs listening to everything.

Hayden's mother called my dad and asked him not to press charges. After a while, I finally admitted to my parents that we were having sex. The living room buzzed with uneasy energy as my parents, Hayden, and I settled onto the worn couch that had faded fabric from years of use. I was seventeen when I bravely shared my truth with them.

My mother's footsteps echoed softly on the floor as

she walked to the kitchen with her tense demeanor on display. Once she was inside, I could hear the rustle of papers. When Mom returned, her face was set with determination as she placed a calendar on the table in front of us. The colorful squares stared up at us, each date a reminder of responsibilities and looming deadlines. She folded her arms, let her gaze sweep over us, and seemingly searched for understanding. It felt as if she was summoning the weight of our lives at that moment, with each box on the calendar heavy with unspoken expectations and plans. "Pick a date," she said. "When are you getting married?"

The more I tried to escape the fate of being a wife with six children, the more I was being pushed in that direction. There was a lump in my throat that wouldn't leave, and I knew that even if I tried to resist, it wouldn't work. I regressed to the good little Mormon girl and did as I was told.

I moved in with Hayden, and our plans for marriage began to take shape amid the confusion of new beginnings. I felt relief because I was out of my parents' house and no longer subject to their rules. Maybe living with Hayden could bring the freedom I yearned for. The days before we were to marry quickly turned into a whirlwind of complications.

Hayden's mother broke up with her boyfriend and decided to stay with us until she found a space of her own. The small apartment felt cramped, especially as his mother took over the living room, sprawled out on the couch, and let her belongings overflow into every vacant corner.

I found myself venting to my parents about the sudden invasion of my mother-in-law's possessions. I felt suffocated by the piles of furniture and plants overtaking the balcony. My parents shared my frustration, and emphasized that as a new couple, we needed our privacy. Tensions rose, and one evening, a huge fight erupted between Hayden and me. Our voices echoed off the walls.

At the age of seventeen, I felt the weight of adulthood crashing down, and when we broke up, it felt as though the world had broken apart. We managed to patch things and stay together. Later that night, I met Hayden's mom sitting on the couch, eyes sparkling with determination.

"You need to put that engagement ring back on her finger," she insisted. She was pushing for a wedding before we even caught our breath. Hayden's mother had married as a teenager; this was normal.

In November 1996, the first semester of my senior high school year, Hayden and I went to the courthouse to get our marriage license. My mother went too. She had to give permission for me to marry since I was under the age of eighteen. My mother felt by marrying me off, she was removing the shame I had caused the family.

Wedding dress shopping with my mother felt more

like a chore than a celebration, and each gown was an uncomfortable reminder of the expectations looming over me. My bridal shower was equally awkward, filled with forced smiles and polite laughter. Balancing wedding plans with my senior year was a delicate dance while trying to find my footing in the Mormon community. It felt absurd to juggle graduation, seminary, and high school after I was married. I often wondered how I had gotten as far as I had.

I remember Hayden's sister mentioning their mother's desire to wear white to the wedding. It was another awkward tidbit of information I didn't need to know. Nearly everything said or done had a red flag attached, but the course was set. We were forced to proceed at the insistence of Hayden's mother and my parents.

A day before our nuptials, Hayden's mother was persuaded to wear a red dress. Hayden's mother and my parents placed many expectations on our marriage. Our parents were relentless in their pushing and prodding and making what should have been a joyful time feel like a series of obstacles I never desired for myself.

On the Calendar

My wedding day was a perfect mess. The weather provided a backdrop to a marriage day that should never have occurred. My nerves were shot, and I couldn't tell my left from right. It all felt wrong, but I was obedient. Whether I wanted to or not, I was getting married. Most of the day sped by, filled with errands to run and preparations made to transform me into a blushing bride. Internally, there was a battle of right and wrong, good and bad, and lead or follow consuming my mind and spirit. There was no clear winner or loser; it was more like a violent game of tug-of-war where either option would traumatize me further.

I sat in the manicure chair, getting my nails done, numb to my surroundings. Hearing the uplifting banter of others, I wondered if I would ever feel that way about my life. From the outside looking in, everything looked right. Strangers I passed that day congratulated me on my nuptials, but every well-wish felt like another nail in my coffin. It felt like I was being buried alive and willingly walking to my gravesite. I had not chosen to marry or even shown excitement about the idea, but I knew there was no backing out. Although it was forced, I allowed everything to take place, from the nail salon to the hair stylist. All I could do was go through the motions, numb my true feelings, and suppress my will to run from it all.

When I arrived at the church, it felt like I was a child playing dress-up. It was surreal. I was inside a room with my mom nearby, bawling her eyes out. My mother was not shedding tears of happiness because she was letting go of her youngest child. The event was a spectacle that even she didn't want for me. I watched as her friend consoled her. I could see the sadness in my mother's eyes, but what could I do about it? This was a choice she made for me, not with me. I'm not going to heaven, was all I could think. I knew deep down she wanted something better for me. Hell, I wanted something better for me! The flute soloist's rendition came to an end, and that was the cue for groomsmen and bridesmaids to prepare to enter.

It was everyone's cue. My mother dabbed her eyes with tissue and composed herself. She stared downward as she took her place, hoping to reclaim her dignity before entering. The guests stirred in their seats, and some craned their necks to see if the ceremony was about to begin. A few guests exchanged murmurs and glances. The wedding procession stumbled forward, unsure whether it was time to start. They walked before the flute finished; it was too soon. When the bridesmaids and groomsmen walked to the front of the room my mother yelled, "Go back; you're too early!" The bridal party walked out of the Relief Society room and back into the hallway. Hayden's best friend, who was also his best man, was confused by my mother telling them to go back.

The day was already ruined, everything that didn't go smoothly only confirmed the idea that I should not be there. Marriage wasn't the answer, but no one was willing to have a conversation with me; they only wanted to make demands. It was painful to see and even more painful to endure without being able to say a word. My dad looked at me with pity while I cried. I gazed down the church hallway with its carpeted walls and wanted to run through the glass doors, but I was frozen in place. I felt cold and suffocated. My legs were firmly planted. I was determined to patch up my "good Mormon girl," status. It was awful.

My bridesmaids, each dressed in a pink lace gown, looked either miserable or confused. The atmosphere of the room had no joy. I walked toward the front pew, the thickening silence weighing against my lungs. I felt winded. Hayden's face was contorted with misgivings. He had an angry face when the bishop said during the ceremony that we would not be in the same phylum because Hayden was not Mormon.

Hayden and I married at the Mormon Church on Wednesday, November 27, 1996. It was the day before Thanksgiving, and my senior year in high school. Rather than warmth, there was a fake festive spirit. After the ceremony, a small line of family and close friends offered us quick, hollow congratulations. Everyone was somber, and maybe it was the right occasion for it.

My friends gave me a halfhearted hug and a look of pity. I didn't want to be in that situation where no one wanted me to get married. Our wedding was not the cheerful occasion Mormons advertised during my entire youth. The marriage felt empty and full of unknown challenges that would not wait to rear their heads. Hayden also didn't want to get married, yet we were two young people who pledged fidelity to each other as if we knew what those words meant. We stumbled around at the reception, trying to make the best of a bad situation. We danced and tried to find other ways to lighten the mood with our friends. As soon as we left the reception, walked out of the church, and shut the doors of his car, the screaming began. Hayden rolled down the window as he drove out of the church parking lot and threatened to throw out his wedding ring.

Hayden would not make decisions without his mother's blessing, and I felt he would not have gotten married had she not condoned it. It was hard to ignore how her presence seemed to guide his every choice; her voice was always the first he'd listen to.

His mother married when she was fifteen, had Hayden when she was seventeen, and then her daughter at nineteen. For him, getting married at twenty was better than getting married at fifteen. It was as if getting married was a rite of passage he was overdue to complete. It was a task he was willing to shoulder since he was five years older compared to his mother. I am grateful that Hayden's mother didn't want him to join the Mormon Church, since that would have made circumstances more challenging.

We honeymooned in San Antonio. We planned to spend Thanksgiving in Houston with family, so we decided to stay at a hotel in Houston. From the moment we left the wedding and through most of the night at the hotel, we argued. There was not a minute in our marriage that was free of tension. It had gotten so bad that we were ready to get a divorce, and we hadn't yet been married one hour! I'm not sure how we made up or if we made up at all.

Both families were supposed to come together to celebrate Thanksgiving. Hayden's sister and his mother were planning to have the celebration at my relative's house but decided to go to a friend's house at the last minute. My family went to my sister's in-law's house. There was lots of noise, and my family and my parents got in the middle of things they should have stayed out of. Hayden and I tried to tell my mom how the bishop had been rude during the ceremony, but she blew us off. It was another day of frustrations, interruptions, and conflicting emotions. Each moment was filled with simmering grievances and unspoken resentments. It was a toxic and unhealthy environment. It was another burden on a young couple attempting to integrate both sides of their dysfunctional families.

Because I was so young, I blamed my parents for forcing me to get married. Under their leadership, I found myself in a space I was not ready for. They should have known better and guided me in a way that would enable me to make better choices, but of course, hindsight is always 20/20. Instead, I was forced into a tumultuous relationship and wondered if I had the strength to undo such a thing. 'Wife' was a title that didn't fit me any second of any day. I was a girl, and he was a guy, and we were playing in a real-life house.

After the holiday break, I returned to high school as a wife. It was liberating to be a seventeen-year-old girl living in an apartment with a husband. I had my own space and felt I had a say over what would happen in my life. I used my newfound independence as any adolescent would, to have a good time. I invited my friends over to smoke weed and hang out without the restrictions my parents had placed on me.

Although it was the first time I didn't need to worry about my parents' reaction to my life, my husband's reaction was the same. Most of our fighting was over me smoking, and I found that I was bound from being myself even from him. It was like I was still living with my parents, and it made me resentful.

Hayden's full-time job and my part-time job did not meet our financial needs. We struggled to maintain our finances, and although we had adult responsibilities, neither of us was ready for this commitment. We didn't know how to communicate with one another. Solving problems was not at the forefront of our minds. Blame and discontent surged us forward and then backward constantly. Our relationship had been stretched beyond our understanding. The realities of adulthood and paying bills had sunk in.

With the bills piling up and Hayden needing surgery, we reached our financial breaking point. We asked to move in with my parents and they agreed. The night before his surgery, Hayden's mother came to help pack the apartment. I remember her rummaging through my kitchen, throwing things in boxes quickly. She had changed residences so much that it was second nature; watching her also overwhelmed me. I didn't want to get used to packing up and starting over again.

Hayden and I were two kids playing at being adults,

tangled in a marriage we didn't know how to nurture. Arguments flared as easily as a match striking dry tinder. Each word was a spark that fed the fire. All these years later, memories of our immaturity flood my mind. There were rare moments of reflection that could've helped me grow, but I was stuck in my own cyclone of destruction. Hayden was on the same cycle and riding on his own track.

I recall that I lashed out and hit Hayden one night as we argued. He didn't hesitate to retaliate. He pinned me against the car door in an instant. I felt the cool metal pressing into my back as his hands gripped my shoulders firmly enough to hold me there without hurting me. "Don't ever touch me like that again," he said, his voice low and steady. At that moment, he displayed the kind of calm that cut deeper than yelling.

His demand was fair because, as much as we had gone back and forth with words, we had never laid hands on each other. The altercation ended, but that didn't stop me from discussing it with my mother. Maybe I secretly hoped to get her to see the truth; we didn't need to be married. Maybe then she would make the executive decision to make it all go away and I could live my life like a teenager again. Instead, she told me I needed to see a therapist, which I also thought was a fair request.

***

My brother was living on the streets. He came to my parents' house to steal food from the refrigerator and tools from the garage. My husband and I were living in the dining room, which had been converted to a bedroom and was next to the fridge. I was aware of how my brother behaved when he was high and didn't want any more turmoil in my life. I was afraid he would get violent, and I locked the back door to keep him outside. I remember that he took a hammer to the front door and pounded on it repeatedly. That's the last thing I remember.

My mother's recollection of that day was that Hayden called the police, and they arrested my brother. She still sounds as resentful in 2024 as she did the day it happened. Her voice was tight and disappointed as she whispered, "Did you have to call the police? He's already in enough trouble." Her continued script about doing whatever was necessary to keep the peace was confusing. For years, my mother was mad at me because my brother went to jail. Somehow, it was my fault that my brother threatened me with a hammer.

I went from fighting with my brother to fighting with my husband. Once, when we went to the movies, I leaned over the seat and kissed him. I didn't notice the people, but he did. He got quiet and then started yelling at me. At

63

some point, the arguing ceased, or maybe we both just gave up, I'm not sure. I just know we'd argue, it'd be over, and then the next argument began.

The rhythm of our relationship was a constant cycle of fights and fragile truces, with each reconciliation shorter than the last. Eventually, I'd begun picturing a future with children trapped in the crossfire, their lives tangled in our arguments. Hayden's voice became a daily force; rising, falling, frustration turning to shouting that wore me down. My spirit was eroding like acid on metal. I'd just turned eighteen and graduated from Windfern High School. I was too young to be married, yet there I was, feeling old and cornered.

Depression was creeping in, and my mother encouraged me to go to couple's therapy with a therapist who was Mormon and had helped other women in the church. Hayden was unable to attend the first session, but my mother drove me so I could attend the couple's session alone. I talked about how we fought every day. He yelled, broke picture frames, and pushed me when we argued. The therapist recommended I read Men Who Hate Women and the Women Who Love Them. She handed me a slightly worn paperback, its title practically shouting from the cover. I flipped through the book and decided that the words felt too raw, too close to my emotions. I didn't open the book that day, but I wish I had. Twenty years passed before I finally read the book. How different would things have been had I stayed in Houston and continued therapy? Therapy might have helped me to see myself and the path I was on clearly, but I was not ready then.

Hayden got upset when he saw that book and made sure to attend the second session with me. Hayden told the therapist how I hit him, after which she told both of us that we mustn't physically fight. Walking out of the office, Hayden looked vindicated, his broad shoulders peacocked and arrogant. The therapist said it would take five years of therapy for us to heal as a couple. I told my mother I couldn't do it.

My parents were pressuring Hayden to convert to Mormonism and meet with the missionaries for the discussions. Us living with them made it hard to avoid adding tension to an already stressful relationship. Hayden decided that after I graduated, he wanted to move to East Texas and live in a trailer in the back of his mother's house. He wanted to be away from my parents pestering him and wanted his mother's support. I didn't want to move to East Texas.

One Sunday, seven months into the marriage, I skipped church. My parents were concerned and came to talk to me. I crumbled under the weight of it all, letting the truth spill out that my attendance was not the problem; it was our constant fighting. I felt small and trapped with Hayden. It was all devastating and consuming, and I wasn't sure what to do. "This doesn't feel like love," I murmured, the words sounding strange. "I don't want to be married anymore."

My father granted me a divorce. As my father and I were on our way to Galveston he said, "I'm not going to tell you what to do. My parents forced my sister to get a divorce, and I'm not going to do that to you. It's up to you if you want to get a divorce."

The final breaking point was a fight on my eighteenth birthday. We were supposed to be celebrating my day. I only wanted a few hours of fun and lightness, but the gap between us had grown to be an uncrossable divide. 'Adulting' was already a burden we were barely managing. Even then, we couldn't find common ground. He muttered about money that day and how we couldn't afford to splurge.

Twenty-five days later, I packed my things and moved to Idaho to live with my grandmother. Hayden's memory trailed me. It was a confusing mix of feelings; good moments that felt faded, distant, and bad ones that sat heavy in my chest. He'd been my best friend, someone I thought I'd love forever, but the truth settled in. The relationship was a poison I needed to leave behind. Hayden moved to his mother's place in East Texas.

I gathered every picture I had of him and threw it all away. Cleaning out the last remnants, I took off my wedding ring and handed it to my mom. "You and Dad paid so much for me. Sell it if you want," I said. I didn't want to owe them, and I didn't want the ring as a reminder. My dad and I packed up and drove north, the miles stretching between me and a life I was finally ready to leave behind.

Trying Something Different

It felt that I would never be forgiven for my transgressions and for living in sin. Instead of dealing with them, I fervently distanced myself from my problems and drew closer to plausible solutions. Leaving Texas and going to Idaho was the solution; I was willing to try and begin again.

I was merely going through the motions after leaving Hayden. My mind understood why we shouldn't have ever married, but I felt lost without him. During that same time, my father wrote letters and told me he wanted to bring the family together more often. He felt we needed to have more fun and share experiences to strengthen our emotional and spiritual bonds.

While I was beginning to live my internal struggles out loud, my brother was in jail, and he had only forty-seven days left in his sentence. Coincidentally, our family had a reunion that summer in Idaho, which benefitted my father's goal. He offered his children family dinner every Sunday night at 5:30 and encouraged us to take advantage of the opportunity. He felt it was important to keep our family ties close even after we were adults. I read the letter and shrugged my shoulders, unsure if these efforts would be enough to strengthen the ties that bound us.

I was a shell of myself and wasn't quite sure what to do. When my grandmother kicked me out of the house, my father chose to come back to Idaho to set me up in an apartment near Rick's college. Living off-campus in an apartment with other girls was short-lived, and I moved to Idaho Falls to attend a satellite class at Idaho State University. Going to college was an attempt to obtain forgiveness for my sins, as if this would be the end of my struggles, but I found myself unable to shed the burdens of my past. I began partying, doing drugs, and drinking while still an avid cigarette smoker. I didn't really drink daily before I enrolled in college, but I found some solace from shame and disappointment when I was intoxicated. Drinking was the only way I could drown out the negative self-talk, fears, and traumas that I had been unable to sweep under the rug.

After moving into my own apartment, I met a guy. He was rough around the edges, had unkempt hair, a half-smirk that never quite reached his eyes, and a restless energy that hinted he was trouble. Against my better judgment, I agreed to go camping with him. We drove up into the mountains, leaving behind the hum of the city for the thick quiet of the pines. By the time we found a spot to set up, we were deep in the woods, miles from the nearest trailhead, with only the towering evergreens and the faint sound of a creek for company.

As we pitched our flimsy tent under the darkening sky, a strange mix of thrill and unease settled over me. The air was damp and heavy with the scent of moss and pine sap, and the fading sunlight cast long, twisted shadows that seemed to move when I wasn't looking. He laughed a little too loud, popped the top on a beer, while I drank MD 20/20. His eyes gleamed in the half-light as if this whole scene was some grand adventure. Beneath his laughter, I could sense a brittle hollowness that pricked my skin.

We sat in silence as the stars began to blink awake. Surrounded by the endless dark of the woods, it was just the two of us, isolated and small in the vastness of the mountains. I wrapped my arms around my knees, ignoring the growing sense that maybe I'd made a mistake going out with him. When he leaned in to kiss me, I accepted the affection. It was nice to feel someone's warmth even if I didn't feel the same way.

The kissing turned to heavy petting without any words, and it seemed that as I pulled away, he pushed further into me, not allowing me to speak. His face pressed haphazardly against mine. I knew where this was leading, but I wasn't in the mood. He wanted to have sex. I remember thinking, I don't know if he will stop if I say no. I went along with it because I didn't want to get hurt.

There was no way I was going to come away from this moment unscathed. I was damned if I did, and afraid to find out how damned I'd be if I didn't. This was not what I wanted, but I didn't want it to turn into some violent encounter where no one could hear my screams. I did not want to be a rape victim.

***

An envelope and letter sat on the end table in my apartment as I packed for a trip to Washington State with my boyfriend, Donnie. My new relationship helped to mask my concerns for a little while, but of course, it didn't solve anything. There were some brighter days intertwined with the darkness. I did gain a new perspective on intimacy. It was the first time I enjoyed sex. Orgasms were the doorway through which I walked to finally appreciate my femininity. For the first time, I felt empowered by something that had only compounded my shame before. I realized that sex can be enjoyable for women, too.

Donnie's father had passed, and though I wasn't feeling well, I wanted to support him during his time of loss. The stomach pain that gnawed at my side for the past week was a quiet hum compared to the need to be there in a friend's time of need. I brushed off the pain,

71

telling myself it could wait until we returned. I thought the pain was related to my period since I had not had it for months.

The drive back to Idaho from Washington was uneventful until a sharp, searing pain tore through my abdomen, forcing me to double over in the passenger seat. Every bump in the road felt like fire. A hospital sign loomed on the roadside, and I pointed toward it, urging Donnie to follow. He was clearly concerned and followed directions to a tee until we arrived at the entrance. Inside the hospital, the air smelled of disinfectant and urgency, but the answers they gave me were wrong. They made a quick diagnosis, wrote me a prescription for antibiotics, and made a dismissive mention of a venereal disease that I knew I didn't have.

My pain didn't waver. Hours later, transported by ambulance, I was moved to a larger hospital in Eastern Washington. The cycle repeated: give the tests, antibiotics, another woman's exam and wrong conclusions. By the time they finally wheeled me into exploratory surgery, my appendix was perforated and poisoning me from within. I needed an ostomy, but they didn't want to do it because of my age. It was an emergency, and they had to perform the first procedure.

Two days later, I was back to the operating room to undergo the second surgery. The nurse informed me that my mother was on the phone. I was strongly sedated and can't remember the conversation we had except that the physicians told my parents I wasn't going to make it. My sisters even reached out to me while I was there.

"Your mother is on the phone," the nurse said, handing me the receiver. I remember saying, "Mom, this isn't a good time to talk." The rest of the conversation was a blur intertwined with the trauma of the moment and the sedatives they'd given me. What did stick out about the conversation was how my mother's voice cracked like glass beneath the weight of her worry. My parents traveled over a thousand miles on a Greyhound bus from Houston, Texas, to Wenatchee, Washington, carrying fear that was heavier than their luggage. Another two days passed, and my lungs collapsed during the second surgery. Machines hummed in the ICU as I drifted between lucidity and a fog of medication. A nurse leaned over me; her voice was soft but urgent.

When I awakened, my mother sat by my side, wiping my forehead with a cool cloth and whispering quiet reassurances. It was a strange and humbling experience to have her care for me like that. I was in the hospital for another week completing follow-up procedures, consultations, and receiving updates on my eventual discharge.

One evening, the doctors gave us permission to go off campus for a few hours. My parents drove me to the top of a beautifully decorated forest ridge. It was a sight that would confirm for any non-believer that only a higher power could have created such beauty and splendor. Once we reached the top, I was ready to enjoy the air and listen to nature, but what happened next was beyond my understanding. My parents immediately inundated me with a barrage of questions.

"What happened?"

"Why are you acting like this?"

"What are you doing?"

"Did you have an abortion?"

"Why are you so depressed?"

They went on, and on, and even further. I refused to say a word. I shut down, froze to protect myself, and stonewalled them as best I could. It was too much; they kept pestering me, question after question. After twenty minutes of bullying me with their worries, they gave up, and we drove back to the hospital.

The Mormon missionaries who visited my hospital room prayed over me. Their hands were warm on my head as they spoke words of blessing. My surgeon, also a Mormon, told me with a grave smile that I needed to return to the church. His tone was firm, and his words were as invasive as the surgeries that had saved my life. His words did not have the same effect as the surgery had.

I was finally discharged. Knowing that I would leave the hospital and return to Idaho was slightly comforting. My father went to retrieve my car from the parking lot and pick us up at the entrance. When he unlocked my car and got in, he found a bra lying on the back seat. As soon as he pulled to the entrance where I sat waiting in a wheelchair with my mother, I saw the look on his face.

"I know what you're doing in here," he yelled, clearly upset. He opened the door for me, and my body ached in protest as I eased myself into the back seat. It was no longer my car; we all got in and began the drive to my place in Idaho.

The gentle hum of the engine underscored the tentative atmosphere. The air was heavy with unspoken concern as Mom checked the rearview mirror for the fifth time before pulling onto the highway. My dad was in the passenger seat. It was a very challenging night driving back to Idaho. The miles stretched ahead, and the road was a blur of gray asphalt and green countryside.

My mother kept stealing glances at me. Her fingers curled and uncurled around the steering wheel as if she was resisting the urge to reach out. My father stared out of the window looking as though he was about to burst. I could see the tension in his eyes, but there was nothing I could do to relieve his agitation. The pressure to be perfect was the furthest thought from my mind. Although I still longed to please my parents, I didn't know how to consolidate their version of me with my true self.

When we arrived in Idaho, the news of my uncle's passing landed as if it were a heavy stone, sinking into the already turbulent waters of my life. When it rains, it pours, and it seemed that my dad was being struck from all sides. Dad flew to California, leaving Mom and me at Grandma's in Idaho.

The air in my grandmother's home was thick with quiet and grief, but my mom's presence made the air feel lighter. We were without my father, and it felt like we were friends. The tension from my father no longer dragged us down. We enjoyed each other's company for a while. My mother went through her old record collection and found something to play. My mother and I sat on the living room floor together listening to her old Elvis Presley records; it felt that we were teenagers living in the 1950s. As the needle found its groove, the room filled with his voice; rich, haunting, and alive. The music carried a strange comfort, a link to something timeless and untouched by the chaos swirling around me. In that moment, I wasn't just listening to Elvis, I was holding onto a piece of something simple, something real; my mom was my friend.

When my father returned from the funeral, we all drove to Houston. They didn't want me to recover alone, or maybe it was a way for them to keep me close and monitor my behavior. Regardless of their reasoning, I needed assistance after two surgeries. Once we were in Houston, my parents asked me to talk to the bishop. The weight of their expectations filled the small space between us, and I sank deeper into the living room chair. The thought of a conversation with the bishop added another layer to my already fragile recovery. It left me raw, not just from physical scars but from the fragility of life, health, and the thin threads connecting me to those who'd rushed to my side when everything fell apart.

After My Appendectomy

July 13, 1998 – Journal writing:

Can your soul truly be saved? Bishop Smith says that everything I have done to myself can be forgiven. He asked if I had ever killed anyone. Of course, I said No. He looked at me with eager eyes and said not to worry because I could be forgiven, but how can my soul be forgiven after seven years of sin? I'm not happy having sex and doing drugs, but how do I stop? I feel I have a creative side that I have not explored. I don't want to be alone. I think having sex makes me feel loved, but I don't love these men. They are just toys. I am toying with men's emotions because I am on the fence about learning to be Mormon, wanting to be Mormon, or staying a sinner.

It took me a solid six weeks to heal from the physical scars, but I still masked the mental and emotional ones with drugs, alcohol, and sex. I wasn't happy, but I didn't know how to stop. I was so full of shame that I constantly criticized myself. My insides were warring, and I was unsure which side I was on…mine or mine. My fears created a narrative that said I was not going to the highest level of Heaven, and that I wasn't pure enough to marry in the temple. These thoughts only added to my anxiety and need for substances, which made everything worse. The drugs numbed me while the sex made me feel loved. I continued to use men as toys while I tried to figure out if I was going to become a Mormon or stay a sinner.

Life pushed forward, yet I felt stagnant living a life that declared women were only meant for obedience. Meanwhile, the boys I'd grown up with were coming back from their missions, radiating a sense of purpose I couldn't muster. I was still drifting, tangled in my own mistakes, and knotted in an existence that only further perpetrated my sense of worthlessness. This fed the misgivings I had about myself and who I could become.

My brother had returned from jail, his eyes heavy with something I couldn't name. He moved like a man carrying invisible weights, and true to my upbringing, my focus shifted to him entirely: his pain, his struggle. I thought of ways to ease his burden and pushed my own issues further into the background. I faded once again into the tapestry of our childhood family dynamic.

The practice of men being more important consumed me daily. I was attending church again, although I still avoided taking sacrament. One Sunday, as my mom sat beside me, I noticed her hands folded neatly in her lap. It wasn't until the light caught her left hand that I noticed it: my wedding ring. It glinted on her finger, a bold contradiction to the tension she'd always held toward Hayden. My stomach knotted as I stared at it trying to understand why she'd wear my wedding ring.

The service droned on, but my mind was elsewhere, caught between the strangeness of her choice and the unease it stirred in me. When I questioned my mother later, she admitted she was wearing my wedding ring because dad accidentally threw hers away. Mom had gained weight and was unable to wear her ring comfortably. She had put her ring under the trash bag in the trash can to hide it from my brother who would pawn it and buy drugs. My dad cleaned the room and threw out the trash, not realizing my mother had hidden her ring there. Her quiet confidence as she wore it was a puzzle I couldn't solve. It was a piece of her reasoning just out of my reach. I finally let it go since I was unable to resolve it.

I found a job at a Denny's Restaurant and met this girl while working there. She offered me heroin. I declined but found that I needed a friend to hang out with. With her, there was no judgement, and it was easy to be toxic around those who were in the same spot I was in. I went with her over to her friend's house, which was right across from my brother's friend. It was a huge party place. I became friends with my brother's friends and began dating Jason, who sold pot to smoke crack. It didn't seem that bad since he had a full-time job, an apartment, and a car. He had his shit together.

It was after I met him that I first snorted heroin. He had cooked up some black tar. I watched them snort it and thought it was okay since they weren't using needles. I tried it; and I hated it. I laid on the living floor unable to talk to my friends, and then spent the rest of the night in the bathroom puking my guts out. I couldn't move. The next night, I hung out with the same 'friends' and tried cocaine for the first time. I knew cocaine would be my new best friend after my first try. My weekends consisted of using coke and then taking benzos to sleep after a night of partying.

I only partied on weekends. I felt that going to school and working during the week slightly redeemed me and my nonsense. I was certain that I would not turn out to be a junkie like my brother; though I was smoking, drinking, taking pills, using cocaine and ecstasy.

After a night of snorting coke, I drove back to my parents' house and took some Z Bars so I could sleep. When I walked through the back door, my mom and brother were headed to work. My brother was sober and feeling especially arrogant that day. He said, "Look, Mom, Crystal's doing what I used to do." He said it to get under my skin, but I was in no mood to battle. I went to bed.

I worked two part-time jobs, went to school, and still found time to party while living at my parent's house. I was young and thought this was a rite of passage.

I hit my bottom when I went into a closet, stole my sister's flute, my brother's saxophone, my coronet and trumpet and pawned them for money to buy drugs. I crossed the line. I turned into my brother. My mother told me to either go to church or Alcoholics Anonymous. In 2000, I moved back to Idaho thinking a change in cities would solve my problems.

No Footing

My life was in a constant state of turbulence because of me or due to outside forces. I had become accustomed to chaos, thriving in its drama and shrieking from its drain. On one hand it felt good to live life without judgment or guilt, but when the high wore off, I was even heavier than before. The revolution was as concrete as the Earth around the sun. It was a movement that was spirit crushing and unnoticeable until I reawakened from another blackout. I couldn't deal with myself, so I hid behind the pills and partied.

I am unsure if I was looking for stability at that time. Was I content with the rush of the 'here and now?' I found a modest apartment in Pocatello right across from a university. I had no luxuries, no local television or cable, and I would often go to other places to distract myself from self-reflection. The clink of bottles at the nearby bar often filled the quiet of my mind an provided me with company as I retreated from myself. The taste of adulthood untethered from supervision and religious boundaries presented a false sense of confidence that was exhilarating.

Kirsten, a lively neighbor in my complex, quickly became my partner-in-crime. By 4 o'clock we were at the bar causing a ruckus or mixing it up at someone's place. Laughter fueled our nights as we plotted our next adventure, listened to music, and revealed in the sharp tang of cheap booze. I was twenty-one years old and truly learning what it was like to be an adult out on my own.

I fiercely clung to the idea of living life on my terms and chasing freedom with every reckless decision I made. My declaration of independence was to indulge in the substances that provided the haze I craved. While those I grew up with dreamed of weddings and nursery rooms, I toasted rebellion and wrote my own prescription for my daily existence.

There was a huge part of me that really wanted to do better and wasn't sure how to make it happen. I figured if I moved away from the people who enabled my behavior, I could slowly get my life together.

Problem Drinking-April 15, 2001 - *Journal writing*:

It was the first Easter away from my parents. I moved up to Idaho a year ago to become Mormon once again. It took one Sunday session to say that it sucks ass. I finally realized that organized religion is complete bullshit. I'm tired of feeling guilty for no reason except for the fact I'm not following a certain set of rules. I've been single since December, and it feels great to be independent from a man. I'm usually at the bar right by my house…I think I'm developing a drinking problem that I need to get control of.

The drinking went to extremes quickly. I hadn't escaped anything. My nights blurred together while I spent my days recovering instead of attending classes. Each night I was more out of control than the last, and each day I spent trying to make up for the losses of not attending class. I thought blacking out was normal and just another part of drinking. *Doesn't everybody black out?*

School was important, but the freedom of choice became my addiction. Not being a Mormon felt more liberating. In the beginning, I did just enough at work and school to get by, but I was having a hard time maintaining as the drinking became more of a habit. Once, I found myself at some guy's house and freaked out after taking a bong rip.

Panic arose when I glanced around and realized that I was the only woman in a room full of guys. I ran out of the house screaming, with the adrenaline drowning out any sense of shame.

My life was unraveling. Attending class was no longer something I was concerned about. I was accomplishing nothing in school or in life. I was nearly expelled from school after I strangled my boyfriend in the dorm. We drank, we fought, he threw a boot at my head and called me names. Idaho felt suffocating, and I was lost. It was the worst place for me to be. I was living in hell surrounded by Mormons and drunks.

I was sinking into debt and barely made it through school. I used the money my parents gave me for tuition to buy alcohol. I was being completely immature about my finances, my health, and my relationships. I thought the geographic, rural life just wasn't for me, and I needed to distance myself from the Mormon community. In another act of defiance, I got a beautiful tattoo of a fairy on my back. Little did I know that it would be such a painful process that I couldn't finish it in one sitting. I returned three weeks later to allow the artist to complete the coloring.

Amid the mayhem, I got the opportunity to work in a program that gave me clarity and enlightened my path. I worked as a counselor for high-risk teens, where high school students had a chance to live in dorms and catch up on their academics to graduate high school. My goal at the time was to become a schoolteacher. I believed the program would present a perfect opportunity for me to get my feet wet and understand the career better. I sat in classrooms and observed while teachers wrangled with students who had behavioral issues. I soon realized that teaching wasn't for me; however, the workspace provided the opportunity for me to counsel students after school. I found myself drawn to deeper-level human connections. It was the first time I had clarity about my purpose and how it would benefit me in my future. I saw what I didn't want my future to look like and embraced the hope of gaining a better understanding of myself. A focus began to clarify itself and formulate its way into my consciousness though I had already run out of options to remain in college.

After a year, I returned to my parents' home and enrolled at Houston Community College. My intention was to get a job and pay my tuition, but I was unable to. My parents paid my tuition again. Their willingness to bail me out only deepened my resentment, anger, and confusion. I faulted them for using financial means to control me. I used all my energy to hate the church and the stupid men who held authority over me. I felt my life should not be subject to a man's control or anyone else's except my own. I was angry that the church allowed men to say and do whatever they wanted, but I, simply because I was a woman, was tethered. I was bitter because men were exalted at the top of the hierarchy. I detested the idea that men ruled over women and wielded control with impunity while women had to be submissive and silent.

What I detested most was that the Mormon church allowed domestic violence to occur. There were no consequences for men's violent behavior, and women walked a narrow path in negotiating it.

My agitation extended so far that I couldn't see clearly or objectively. I was determined to write my own rules, whether they were acceptable to others or not.

One part of me wanted to put the past behind me and shed the negativity like old skin, while another part of me clung to the trauma because the sharp edges were familiar. Instead of running toward healing, I leaned further into what was easier. My brother and I had begun partying together frequently. We were both drinking and drugging. We graduated to all things toxic and behaved like juveniles with no regard for our adult responsibilities and consequences. Recklessness became our shared language as we rekindled our childhood bond. We were two peas back in the same pod, or in our case, our father's garments.

One day while we were living at our parent's house, my brother and I ran out of beer. We went to the gas station where I worked and stole some. My coworker called the house, and dad went to pay for it. Dad was the constant enabler to our shenanigans. Just as is the case in many families that have relatives with addiction, our father presented rescuing behaviors instead of allowing us to endure the consequences of our criminal offense. We should have been arrested for stealing. Instead, my dad saved me just as he had saved my brother from the criminal acts he had begun committing at age fourteen. I was too high to recognize dad's rescue for what it really was.

The partying escalated to the point that a guy I was seeing dumped me because he said I drank too much! Though his words hung in the air as heavy and undeniable truths, I still wasn't ready to confront the issue; I was still willing to drown in it instead.

My brother tried to get himself together multiple times. Rehab was a huge part of his disastrous cycle. Some interventions lasted longer than others, but nothing stuck. He'd be right back at his tomfoolery for another round or two, determined to win the fight despite losing every battle.

It was a normal night out for us, hanging out at a motel drinking. My brother's girlfriend was there, and of course, no night was complete without high-impact theatrics. I can't remember what my brother and his girlfriend argued about, but it escalated. Before long, he had hit her, and blood was streaming down her face. There was no panic or concern; it was just another day with my family. I left her in the motel crying and got my brother out fast, because, of course, the person to save was the man. I never failed to revert to my instinct to protect my brother at all costs. I found myself drunk driving my brother home, listening to him cry about not knowing why he hit her. I was rescuing him from the consequences of his behavior. That wasn't his first assault, nor would it be his last.

It was a family affair when it came to spiraling out of control. Close calls one day did not stop us from repeating the same destructive behavior the next day. My brother and I went to the bar to drink with his friends one night. We drank as we always did and laughed until tears fell. We reminisced about previous escapades and gathered ourselves for yet another night of adventure. I left the bar with my brother and his friend, unaware that they were selling ecstasy. I found myself in the familiar position of being unable to make decisions about my own safety and well-being.

I was stuck sitting in a car on the side of the road while my brother and his friend were in the middle of a bizarre drug deal. Even in my stupor I found the events unacceptable and realized I could do nothing about it. My voice meant nothing to my family, so why should I start voicing it then? I talked loudly to myself about how stupid this whole moment was. It was all the defiance I could gather. At no point did I ever think about removing myself from the situation; I did not think to save myself. I had become accustomed to doing what everyone else in my life did: ignore Crystal.

I sat there, powerless to leave, and let the drug deal evolve. My drunken stupor had dissipated and allowed me to think freely and create a safe space. This was something I had never practiced before, and I had no confidence at all that I could pull it off. I retreated instead, into the recesses of my mind, only to be jarred back to reality when the guns appeared.

I thought, "What the f…!" My brother jumped in the car and drove off. I wanted to get out, but I wasn't about to jump out of a moving car. My opportunity had passed. Now, I spent time blaming myself for not shielding myself from whatever was about to transpire and regretting my passiveness. I had nowhere to go; I was along for the ride.

Somehow, we made it out of that situation without any shots being fired. Seconds of fear replaced minutes of carelessness as we drove down the road toward more mischief.

My brother's friend shot the gun through the car's sunroof, my brother slammed into another car, and I thought I was going to die. We escaped one near death experience only to be jolted into something else entirely. Enough was enough. I yelled at my brother to pull over as my hand gripped the door handle. He yelled back that I was not getting out. He spoke too soon, because blue lights behind us began flickering to signal that the joy ride was over.

The cops pulled us over, spotted the guns and drugs in the car, and hauled us off to jail. I was relieved to be going to jail. I thought I could survive a night in jail but would probably lose my life if I spent another second in the car with my brother at the wheel. My brother and I sat in the back seat of the squad car. I was almost entirely sober at this point. My brother leaned over and whispered that he wanted me to blame everything on his friend. What a friend he was!

The three of us sat in our separate cells at the small city jail in Humble, Texas. It wasn't until 2022, as part of his step work, that my brother finally apologized for involving me in that incident.

I no longer wanted to participate in my destructive pattern of rebel rousing, but I didn't know how to remove myself from it. I was used to natural disasters, and family always had its part to play in it. I returned to Idaho hoping things would somehow turn out differently. Like any other addict, I recycled my problems wherever I was because I wasn't dealing with the root cause of my issues.

I moved to Oregon to live with my sister and her husband. We were money poor but rich in spirit. We had fun, and it was a positive time in my life. Money was tight. We had patio furniture in the living room that my sister's husband had taken from the fraternity house next door. We listened to "Love Lines" with Dr. Drew and Adam Corolla on the radio and smoked weed. I was more on track than ever, although partying was still a huge part of who I was.

I drank every day. I rationalized it by saying that drinking is what college students are supposed to do. By

2003, all my partying got me a DUI charge and mandatory substance use disorder treatment. The court order was the first legal consequence I received because of my destructive actions.

Despite the travel back-and-forth from state to state and my drug and alcohol craziness, I completed my undergraduate degree in sociology from the University of Oregon. Earning my degree was the first time I proactively accomplished a goal that had a positive impact on my life and self-esteem. I had been living with my sister and brother-in-law, and I had become really close to them in ways that I had only experienced in short spurts before.

I later moved into a house near campus with two friends. We all went to U of O. I was free from the Mormon shackles and finally learning about myself. We partied like college students, but we also studied like college students. The difference was that I was doing it without shame, which made doing normal things less somber.

On weekends, you could find us at wineries or the local bars. I wasn't married, didn't have kids, and since I was no longer a practicing Mormon, I was free to discover myself at my most basic level.

Graduation day arrived, and my family came to celebrate the milestone. It was such an exciting event for me. Of course, I went out partying the night before. I had finally accomplished something against all odds. I was miserable on graduation day because I was coming down from my cocaine high. The family planned a trip to the sand dunes the day after graduation, but I was too hungover to participate. I stayed behind nursing my pounding head and queasy stomach. My destructive behavior was interfering with my quality of life, one missed moment at a time. I was spiraling and couldn't tell my nose from my foot.

The Valley

As my graduation present, I decided to see the world and do something meaningful simultaneously. Walking the halls at University of Oregon, I saw a flyer for a volunteer program in South Africa. This was my chance to make a difference in the world. I drove back to Pocatello to stay with a friend. The night before my international flight, my friends and I stayed up all night drinking and smoking crack. The next day we drove to Salt Lake City, where I boarded a plane that took me to the East Coast.

I made sure to visit the airport bar while waiting to board my flight to Germany. I quickly learned that alcohol is free on international flights, and that was music to my ears. I boarded my plane for the overseas flight and made sure I took advantage of that free service. I had a twelve-hour layover in Berlin and decided to explore.

The café in Berlin provided me with plenty of time for reflection. I sat there thinking how I never would have believed I'd have an experience like this. It wasn't a Mormon Church mission; it was something I was doing on my own, outside of the church. It felt even more liberating to reflect on this reality. I had created this moment. A man didn't create it. I did.

Traveling through Europe alone gave me confidence I'd never known; however, I was still fighting demons. My demons now had no supplier to feed them. After clearing customs, I returned to the terminal to wait for my flight to Cape Town and saw my reflection in the terminal window. I saw a cracked-out, hollow-eyed restless person exhibiting a blunted affect. I stood at the table, chain smoking nervously, waiting for the next flight, and counting the hours with little thought beyond getting through the moment.

Twelve hours later, I groggily left the plane and stepped into South Africa's humid embrace. I was disoriented but functional. Evidence revealing the time and distance of my flight lay scattered around me. Enough empty wine bottles to fill a medium-size trash bag cluttered my seat. It was a tragic display of my penchant for alcohol. My mind reflected on the scene, but my emotions hurriedly rushed me off to my next destination. Internalizing the contemplative conversation at that moment was impossible.

For the next six weeks, I buried my chaos beneath a façade of purpose and worked with at-risk teenagers in a boy's home. Their lives were marked by loss and struggle, and they emitted echoes of pain I couldn't name in myself. Day by day, I immersed myself in their stories, hoping that my presence offered them something meaningful, even as I battled my own inner turmoil.

The leader of the boy's home was an older man who described himself as a gangster. He used to commit terrible acts of violence, such as setting tires on fire and throwing them over people in an attempt to kill them. When he got sober, he followed a path that led him to believe in Jesus. He belonged to the Christian organization in which I was a volunteer. He said his calling was to help displaced youth and prevent them from making the choices he had made. I hadn't realized when I signed up for the program that I would be expected to attend church on Sundays. I was adamant about not going to church, and I informed them that I was unwilling to participate. The men respected my choice, and it became another moment that silently secured a walk to a healthier path.

The youth facility buzzed with energy. It had a constant hum of creativity and passion. Some boys transformed scraps of their stories into vibrant plays, and they let their voices rise and fall with raw emotion on the makeshift stage. Others strummed guitars or pounded out rhythms on drums; their melodies filled the air with defiance and hope. Art in all its forms spilled from every corner, a painting drying on an easel here, and a dance routine being practiced in the hallway there. The panoply of expressions was a comfortable blanket that melted the ice with which I had encapsulated my heart. I was beginning to feel something beyond negative emotions.

I stood on the sidelines watching in awe as the boys' performances unfolded before me. It warmed my spirit to be part of positive events happening outside of myself. I saw that I could bring positivity to the lives of others. I had been removed from everyone and everything that had me negatively bound. The boys' resilience shone through every note, every line delivered, and every movement made. It was humbling. I experienced moments that continued to push me from my current path into the trajectory of change. I was a witness to a secret inner beauty contained in all mankind. It was as healing for me as it was for those boys.

The colors of Cape Town, the hum of a different language, and the warmth of the people wrapped me in an embracing hug and continued to shatter the walls I'd created in the States. Each new encounter and breathtaking view chipped away at the chaos I carried and gave me room to breathe. Slowly, I began to see my life from a distance; it's disarray sharp, unavoidable, and changeable. The boys, their art, and this unfamiliar place lit a spark inside me I didn't know I was missing.

Volunteering instilled a sense of independence that gave reverence to my inner self. To have the courage to travel to a never-before-seen continent alone at the age of twenty-five showed me my life in a different perspective. I had escaped the Mormon fate for me to be married with three children at that age. Instead of attending the Mormon Church and accepting the patriarch with its enormous limitations, I chose a different path. The trajectory of my life had changed. I had time to reflect, create healthy connections, and spread goodness into the world.

What caused me to consider pausing my regeneration was, after escaping the grasp of a religion into which I was born, I had no idea I had volunteered to serve a different religious organization. This revelation made it harder for me to reconcile my actions with my upbringing. I gained some clarity but was unable to recognize what I was grieving, though I knew I was exactly where I needed to be. I had more work to do to get myself to a continuously peaceful state of mind.

***

When I returned to the States, my patterns led me back to my former state. Drinking once again become a way for me to let loose and have a good time. I was in a new relationship, and the person of interest at the time was another woman. It wasn't the most ideal relationship to have in small-town Idaho. The close-knit community was a large part of what made things hard. I worked with school children who displayed behavioral issues during the day, and at night I was a bartender at one of the two bars in town. With such limiting views, my partner and I looked for a respite. After two years, we packed up and moved to Seattle.

Our relationship was filled with drinking and fighting. It dissolved after the third year, as did many other things in my life, but its end did not stop me from yearning for internal growth and happiness. I was still hanging out, flowing between men and women, until I met Scott. We were both partying and found ourselves drawn to each other. The tie that bound us in the beginning was alcohol.

Our chemistry was undeniable, and it helped that we had the same vice. It was part of our entertainment as a couple and among our friends. Things were progressing well between us when we received shocking news. Scott's best friend passed away from cirrhosis of the liver in 2013. It was a humbling moment, and it began our trajectory of sobriety as a couple when Scott was diagnosed with the same disease a few months later.

On November 14, 2013, Scott got sober. My sober date is five days later, November 19, 2013. Life was still happening around me, as it always had. I was still in debt from school tuition costs, and I was barely paying the bills. Graduate school was stressful, and it caused the onset of debilitating panic attacks. I quit smoking for nearly six weeks, but I found I couldn't maintain it. I took solace in the fact that I wasn't drinking or doing drugs; quitting cigarettes would have to wait.

I began to work through the debilitating Mormon Church ideals, get myself together, and figure out a way to stay sober. I found that sober support meetings were triggering because of their use of scriptures and the Lord's Prayer. The support group told me I couldn't get sober without a God, but at least no one told me what or who my higher power needed to be. If I wanted to go to Heaven, I could choose. That was more autonomy than I had in the Mormon Church.

Journaling was a more comforting process; I began to do more of it and found myself a sponsor. I worked the steps and attended meetings, though I found it exhausting to continue the mental gymnastics when the word "God" came up.

Though I was physically sober, it took years to become emotionally healthy and sober. I was sober and angry all the time. I didn't like being micromanaged at work; in fact, I hated it. It felt that people were always on my ass. My email was packed with advice and lists of things to do or things to stay away from. I just wanted everyone to back off. I went from the Mormon Church and its men who tried to control me to another group of people giving me rules. It didn't help that my sponsor was a born-again Christian. She invited me to church and told me that I needed God; it was not a good match for me. If only I could run away and not deal with any of it anymore.

I went from being uncontrollable in my addictions to having no control in my sobriety. The frenzy wasn't in substances anymore; it lived in my mind and thrashed against the walls I had built. Instead of focusing on my own healing, I fixated on my sponsor. I scrutinized her every word and action. I tore her down in my head to distract from the discomfort she brought me. My judgments didn't stop there. I lashed out at others, criticizing and nitpicking, trying my best to wrest control over something, anything. The silver lining in the cloud of my behavior was that at least I wasn't dissociating.

Day by day, I fought to steady myself. When frustration flared, I paused to breathe deeply until the storm passed. Listening to speakers at meetings was a beacon light; their stories grounded me in a way I desperately needed. My feelings were raw; every slight, real or imagined, stung like an open wound. My ego ached for validation; I needed someone to stroke it and tell me I was wonderful. Instead, I carried such a big chip on my shoulder that it cast shadows over everything.

Work and school were a grind, and stress compounded until I started shutting people out. Overwhelmed, I fumbled through tasks and snapped under pressure. At my job, driving to clients' homes became a daily battle against panic attacks. My boss once called me a pit bull; the words were a sharp rebuke after I wouldn't let go of a coworker's mistakes. He wanted me to calm down, but my stress had reached a boiling point. I grinded my teeth constantly, and I clenched my jaw so tightly I had to force it open to stop myself from cracking a tooth.

There were nights when the thought of drinking whispered in my ear, promising escape. Each time, I faced the weight of my reality instead. Slowly, I found a rhythm; work an eight-hour shift, visit the gym to sweat out my anger, eat a meal that nourishes my body, and attend a meeting that nourishes my soul. My sugar addiction escalated when my control seemed to waiver, but I maintained my sobriety.

In the middle of it all, one bright spot kept me going. For the first time in my life, I was in a relationship with someone who didn't drain me but lifted me. Scott was a kindred spirit. He was someone who understood my battle because he was fighting his own. Together, we clawed our way through our demons, and brick by brick, built a fragile peace in our lives. That harmony felt like safety, and in that safety, I found the strength to keep doing the hard work of rebuilding myself, one day at a time.

Learning to trust myself has been terrifying and liberating. It has been as if opening a door that has been locked for years and uncertain of what lies on the other side. I've found resolution in moments that were once filled with fear. I've learned to make choices without the weight of guilt pressing me down. It has been a long and messy process full of doubt and a series of small victories. With each step forward, I've felt I was reclaiming a lost fragmented piece of myself. I've delved deep to see how I contributed to the unpleasant situations at home and work. I could no longer blame others or the Mormon Church for the state of my life.

Even as I was taking control over my addictions, the panic attacks worsened. At first, driving felt manageable as long as I stuck to the back roads, winding through quiet streets to get where I needed to go, but over time, even that became too much. Fear crept in and slowly took root until I couldn't bear to drive at all. Red lights were my breaking point. In my mind, I had to sit there, trapped in my car with nowhere to go while the two-minute wait stretched to eternity. My stomach churned, my head spun, and I fought the overwhelming urge to fling the door open and leave the running car right where it was, hazards be damned.

Depression followed behind closely, pulling me deeper into isolation. My home became my sanctuary. It was the only place where I felt even remotely safe. Even that solace soon crumbled. The walls that once protected me began to close in, and I shook for hours after a panic attack. Leaving my room felt impossible; the outside world was too overwhelming.

Taco Time became my comfort. Eating "healthy," cheap fast food was a quick way to drown out feelings I couldn't face. I numbed myself with every bite and tried to ignore how far I'd fallen. It took attending months of therapy, doing the grueling work of staying sober, making hard decisions, cutting off toxic friendships, facing fears I'd avoided, and overhauling my entire life before I began clawing my way out. The process was slow. Piece by piece and moment by moment, I rebuilt what my anxiety and depression had stolen. I was no longer using drugs, drinking, or involved in toxic relationships. Now, my choice of poison was eating. I needed comfort, and food was the next addiction to replace all my others.

Without the crutch of substances, I was left alone with my raw, unfiltered emotions, and they overwhelmed me. Panic attacks came in waves, crashing over me until I felt I couldn't breathe. Agoraphobia crept into my life, making even the simplest tasks feel insurmountable. Doctors prescribed antidepressants, and it took months of trial and error before we found the right combination. Benzos dulled the edge but never truly addressed the anxiety until Zoloft was prescribed. Finally, something began to work.

Even so, several years after therapy, working the Steps, having a yoga mat in the closet, and often-untouched anti-anxiety medication in my cupboard, I struggled with consistency. For years, I carried a bottle of Benzos in my purse and stashed extras in my husband's and my car, just in case I had a panic attack. After years of doing self-help books and using the coping skills that I tell my clients, in 2022, I could go on a trip without the benzos.

The hardest part about being sober was dealing with all my feelings. I was no longer dependent on drugs and alcohol. I knew that cigarettes and sugar were unhealthy replacements, but I gave myself some grace. I put down one unhealthy habit and picked up another. When things got too difficult, I kept pushing myself, little by little, to deal with the pieces that needed to be put back together.

Continued Recovery

Recovery is a process; it's waiting for a seed to sprout after planting it in dry, cracked earth. You water it daily, hoping for a sign of green, but growth can remain stubbornly unseen for years. Anything worth having should be worth the effort in creating it, I kept telling myself when progress felt slow. Some days, I woke up with a sense of purpose and almost buoyant with confidence in the process. Those mornings felt as though I was walking outside to a warm, golden sunrise that promised everything would be okay.

Other days were heavy and gray. I'd open my eyes and feel the weight of doubt settle on my chest before I left my bed. Those days dragged and every step forward felt that I was trudging through quicksand. Still, I reminded myself to take one step at a time. Even with the constant push and pull of internal struggles, I was doing well with sobriety. I felt I was breaking out of a suffocating cage and breathing air I hadn't known existed. I felt a fragile sense of control over my destiny for the first time in years. It was oddly intoxicating.

In hopes of getting pregnant, I thought I would stop smoking. "Why not quit smoking, too?" I thought, as if sobriety alone wasn't already an uphill climb.

The first few days were excruciatingly painful. My hands shook, I dropped things, and my temper was short. I'd distract myself with gum, toothpicks, and anything that kept my hands and mouth busy. By the end of the first week, though, it felt like my skin was too tight, and my thoughts crackled like a live wire. Six weeks into the attempt, I hit my breaking point.

I remember sitting in my car, gripping the steering wheel so tightly my knuckles turned white. The anger inside me burned hotter than anything I'd felt in months. I had an unrelenting itch I couldn't scratch. My chest was tight, my head was pounding, and all I could think about was how badly I needed relief. When I finally pulled into the gas station and bought a pack of cigarettes, I tore it open with trembling hands. The first drag felt like a betrayal and a lifeline all at once.

Quitting smoking felt as if I was climbing a mountain with no summit in sight. Maybe I had piled too many goals on myself at once and stacked expectations to the point that they were destined to topple. Sobriety, I could manage. Smoking was something I could not cut out at the time. The pack sat in my pocket as a reminder of my limitations, but I told myself it was okay. Recovery was still a process, and I had plenty of time to figure it out.

At one of the speaker meetings I attended, a man stood at the front of the room mustering the confidence to begin speaking. Once he started though, words poured from his mouth like smooth cream. His voice carried the weight of all the years he spent chasing validation. He shared how he'd been an 'approval sucker.' He described how he would get angry if he didn't get approval from people because his happiness was hitched to a wagon full of weighted goods. I felt that.

My ego got in my way, too. The memory of people flattering me, their words like honey, is vivid. Compliments, sugary and flowing thick, made me feel untouchable and invincible. When I basked in that attention, I smiled and became the kind of person people wanted around. The moment the applause stopped, or the compliments faltered, something inside me twisted. I tried not to show it, but deep down, resentment bubbled up hot and sharp.

I was outwardly blaming everyone for the chip I carried on my shoulder. "They don't understand me," I'd tell myself, as if their perceived slights were why I felt heavy with frustration. I never stopped examining how my actions or mindset contributed to the presence of the chip. The truth was undeniable: my negative thinking was a thick fog I willingly walked with every day. It clouded my judgment, soured my interactions, and darkened my world. As I sat there listening to that man's raw honesty, I realized this was another problem on my ever-growing list that only I could change. It was liberating and terrifying because the solution was within me; it meant taking full responsibility for my quality of life.

When I wasn't flooded with email from work, it was recovery emails continually nagging about one thing or another, outlining tasks I should complete and listing actions I should always avoid. The stress kept me from submitting my work documentation on time, and an intense cycle of chaos continued.

We had been short-staffed, overworked, underpaid, and receiving little praise at work. Even when they did hire someone, there was no consolation. To make matters worse, there was too much hostility at work with the new girl, and I knew the problems would continue. My boss told me I needed to calm down, and my energies were misplaced because I tried to get everyone to like me. I actually wanted to tell everyone to 'F' off, but I knew that wasn't a healthy response.

Patience was a virtue that I rarely considered. I am not a doormat, but I am also not effectively assertive. Learning to speak up for myself was a process that took me years to master. I felt I was constantly being micromanaged by everyone, and I hated it. I carried so much anxiety; I didn't think I would make it. I gained so much weight because my mindset was, at least I'm not drinking or smoking. I clenched my teeth constantly and had to remind myself to open my mouth to release the pressure within.

As if the pressure from the program and work weren't enough, my sponsor was also driving me nuts. Her born-again Christian beliefs consistently rubbed me the wrong way, and there was nowhere to turn for relief. My sponsor was no longer benefiting my emotional sobriety, and the angst I felt every second I was awake created an unsettling atmosphere.

After a long, excruciatingly anxious, stress-filled day at work, I would have to fight traffic to get home. I hated driving on the highway and would avoid it at all costs; taking the long way home only gave my mind more time to race and cause panic. Everything was just moving way too fast. Every time I drove, I'd shake in fear. It was brutal. I had to focus on my physical health as much as I did my mental. I was falling apart at the seams, but I knew I was making progress. There were moments when I was suicidal. I had thoughts of cutting myself or driving off the side of the road. There was my fear of failure, fear of success, fear of being alone, fear of being married, fear of having children, and fear I could not have children. Getting stuck in traffic was the ultimate fear that induced more panic attacks.

My armor was faulty, ruined; really, it was non-existent. I hadn't done anything to protect myself or live to my full capacity; I was too busy hiding to thrive.

I spent days and weeks focusing on whether I would drive and how many places I could go. I'd obsess over a map as if it would eliminate the pending doom and dread of driving. I would pore over route options to avoid the freeway, and though it was the last option, I'd sometimes elicit Scott's help to get me places.

Eventually, I gave up. I stopped driving completely and surrendered to the anxiety that ruled my life. I relied on buses; one to get to grad school and two more to get to work. Each transfer was a small victory and a reminder of how much smaller my world had gotten. I had to learn to function on my own. It was a challenge. It was then that my doctor prescribed Prozac. I went to the urgent care clinic, and the doctor asked if I was suicidal. I lied. I denied having those thoughts because the shame of being a counselor who had those thoughts overwhelmed me. I was a counselor; I was not supposed to be feeling suicidal.

My mind was a cauldron of swirling toxic thoughts that I previously tried to drown out. I found out that toxicity had the gills to survive. Mixed into my pot of fear was getting cancer if I didn't quit smoking, Scott cheating on me, me cheating on him, or my dying. I weighed my thoughts down with such negativity that nothing healthy could grow, and even if it did, it could not flourish. I continued to go to meetings, pray, meditate, and journal.

I felt that I was a fraud for telling my clients to do the cognitive behavioral therapy techniques that I needed to do for myself. I had the same panic attacks that they were trying to overcome. I'd share strategies, but I also worked on those techniques myself. I was a people pleaser which is emotional dishonesty. I could never obtain my goal of unconditional love if I was unable to be my authentic self. I tried to find the will to quit smoking again. I no longer wanted to fit inside the tight boundaries of my childhood. I didn't want to be a people pleaser, take the victim stance, or crouch in a corner where my life happened without my permission.

There was a conflict between the person I was and the person I was choosing to be. I didn't want to be a person who was afraid of everything. I didn't enjoy living with depression; though it was warm and familiar, I knew I could not live there because it made me miserable. Misery led to the behaviors I needed to avoid at all costs.

The anxiety was unbearable. I wanted to be the person who faced everything and recovered from whatever was thrown my way. It seemed that the world was piling on me quickly, and I was buried in the rubble of traumatic garbage from which I could not free myself. I wanted to be a person who shows love to everyone and does not judge people for their character defects.

When things got tough, I wanted to escape. Hard

days at work made me want to digress and drink. Drinking was no longer the solution for me, and I turned to food.

Through meetings and therapy, I learned that when I don't want to feel my emotions, I start thinking about drinking. Nevertheless, I couldn't allow myself to be a coward. I stood taller and stronger every second I dealt with reality instead of running away or hiding behind a vice.

When I slowed down, I'd notice all the wonderful things happening in my life. My bank account flourished, and my car insurance lowered, so I could put that money toward paying off my student loans. My relationship with Scott was the best thing I had going. We both began getting our finances in order to buy a house. We bought the land on which to build our home.

I returned to therapy for three weeks. It was the longest I'd ever gone continuously. The first therapist I saw told me I was a highly sensitive person, which I'd never heard before. The therapist said I am so sensitive that I needed to build armor. My assignment was to read the book, The Highly Sensitive Person. Reading it helped me deal with my anxiety, and I felt it revealed that some situations I'd experienced were normal ones of being an "overly sensitive" child.

Once the antidepressant was in my system for months, I no longer had suicidal thoughts. Attending women's retreats helped me to maintain emotional sobriety and confront the childish, emotional, sensitive, and grandiose characteristics of an alcoholic. These unsavory behaviors all coincided with my being a highly sensitive person.

The medication smoothed the jagged edges of my emotions and dulled the chaos enough for me to feel steady. I clung to the routine of taking it, knowing full well the storm that could break if I didn't. Without it, I was a live wire, snapping at Scott over the smallest things; my inability to control the anger bubbling just below the surface fueled our arguments. Living in the Pacific Northwest didn't help either. The relentless gray skies and the endless drizzle pressed down on me like a suffocating blanket. Day after day, I watched the rain streak down the windows and felt the gloom seep into my bones.

After sixteen months of sobriety, I noticed I still fixated on things, and fear would grab hold. It tore me down and kept me from thinking positively about myself and my future. It was preventing me from obtaining the things I knew were for me. I was in a pattern of passive-aggressiveness and blaming everyone else for my unhappiness.

My bluntness was abrasive. In some ways, it was positive and negative at the same time. My friends said I was the meanest person they liked. What did that really mean? It was a backhanded compliment that helped me continue my pursuit of healthiness. I began to check my motives to gauge whether the compliment was to help or hinder.

I loved myself enough not to damage my body anymore; however, my addictive behavior traveled to binge eating. I began tackling the issue in my journal, where I could force the frankness necessary to heal old wounds. I would not play the Hot Potato game with my addictions. I noticed I didn't clench my teeth as much and the turmoil dissipated into a conquerable hum. My work revealed my flawed way of thinking. It wasn't that I needed to be Pollyanna perfect, but being honest and real with myself and others would help me reach my potential. I deserve love and a wonderful relationship. The only approval I need is my own. I could no longer cut people off or push them away if I wanted to build a community. Running away from being vulnerable was never a solution. The coping mechanisms I used during adolescence no longer served me in adulthood.

In the first year of my recovery, I made amends and apologized to people affected by my destructive behavior, including myself. I looked at myself for who I truly was and accepted the good and the bad. I identified what limited my progress, improved those areas, and enhanced parts of myself that brought me joy.

The second year of sobriety was harder than the first.

The first year is, "DON'T drink, don't DRINK, DON'T F'ING DRINK!" I was haunted by dreams of drinking the entire year. In the dark corners of my mind, the glass of amber liquid gleamed, its surface rippled as if it was alive and calling me. In my dream, in a feeling both familiar and terrifying, I would take a sip and feel the burn sear my throat and settle in my chest. Then I'd wake up gasping with the phantom taste lingering on my tongue. My heart would pound with guilt, and for a split second, I couldn't tell if it was a dream or real. The urge to confess, to pick up the phone and tell my sponsor I'd slipped, was overwhelming, even though I hadn't touched a drop.

The work of recovery began peeling back layers I hadn't known existed. I believed I was kind, giving, and decent for a long time, but that illusion shattered under the bright light of self-examination. The process was brutal. It was as if I was standing naked in a crowded room where everyone could see parts of me I'd tried to hide. Every interaction was a raw exposure where people could look right into the quivering center of my fears and insecurities. My words caught in my throat, my hands trembled during even the simplest conversations, and I felt that my body was not my own.

Despite the constant discomfort, I knew this pain was the price of growth. I had areas of my life that screamed for attention. I had festering wounds that needed tending before they could heal. My recovery wasn't just about abstaining from alcohol; it was about learning to live fully and meaningfully and reach a potential I had not dared to imagine for myself.

Things were slightly easier at home. I had a helpmate. Scott was walking the same path of self-discovery and healing; our shared trajectory gave us a sense of solidarity. We stumbled and argued, but it wasn't physically combative. It was the kind of friction that comes from carving out something better together. Still, the world outside our little bubble wasn't so forgiving. No one cared if I made progress or fell apart; they were indifferent to my struggles. I carried that indifference as a heavy weight, feeling it press on my shoulders every time I stepped outside. It was a reminder that my journey was mine alone, and the path to recovery stretched endlessly before me. There were days when the road felt impossible, with its twists and turns hiding any sign of hope or relief. I knew I couldn't stop. I couldn't let those dreams, those fears, or even the indifferent faces of the world around me derail the fragile progress I had fought to build.

Barren

It was a revelation to learn how much trauma my mother had endured before she ever started a family of her own. I had only seen her through the lens of my perceived shortcomings of her as a parent. Through counseling and step work, I was able to consider what shaped her into the woman she became. When I began the work of making amends, the thought hit me with startling clarity: she had done more for us than anyone had ever done for her.

She had married a Mormon man who didn't drink. It was a deliberate choice that stemmed from the chaos of her own upbringing. In her childhood home, alcohol wasn't just a vice, it was a wrecking ball that smashed through relationships and left emotional devastation in its wake.

Alcohol abuse wasn't the only shadow cast over her life; there were other darker, unspoken traumas that she hinted about on rare occasions. I imagined her younger self, small and scared, navigating a world where safety wasn't a guarantee. That image of her softened the edges of my resentment, though it didn't erase it entirely.

She poured her energy into protecting my brother, her only son. I can still see her fussing over him with quick and purposeful movements, as if shielding him from life's blows was the only thing keeping her upright. In her eyes, he was the apparent heir and future authority of the family. Her favoritism stung and left a quiet ache in the background of my childhood, but as an adult, I began to understand. She was trying to break a cycle the only way she knew how, even if her process was misguided.

My father had a different story. Feelings were foreign territory for him and a place he refused to visit. He existed behind an emotional wall so high and so thick; it was impenetrable. Conversations with him were like watching a movie with the sound off: you could see the action, but you had to guess what it meant.

My first real exposure to therapy came in high school; however, it wasn't for me. It was due to my brother's escalating behavior. I sat across from a psychiatrist in a stiff, uncomfortable chair to get meds. Even then, unsure of what I was supposed to say, I sensed that therapy might hold answers for me, but it wasn't my time. Before I could create a destiny separate from my upbringing, I had a path I needed to walk and lessons I needed to learn the hard way.

I assigned responsibility for my parents' actions to myself for a long time. It was a load I was never meant to carry. Their stuff is theirs; I need to remain hypervigilant with my own growth and development. Even though I still find it hard to separate myself, through it all, I know there is love.

Now that I have detached myself from the past, there is no recourse, no take backs, and no way to blame the effects of my choices on someone else. I couldn't let my old ways affect the new person I'd built. I was more accepting of myself, and it was the best feeling. I figured I could continue to move forward in a positive fashion. There was no reason I couldn't attack any situation with confidence.

My husband Scott is my favorite person, and we have a lot of fun together. I am very fortunate that my husband and I quit drinking together because I have friends for whom that didn't happen. Our ability to allow one another the space to grow and get healthy is what makes us work. I love being around Scott.

It was important for me to continue to walk the path of recovery because I no longer wanted to create chaos. I wanted to enjoy the moment, and life in general, with him. Being with Scott in calmness is priceless, and we work on it every day. For the first time in years, my life was no longer a series of frantic moves from one stat or city to another. The pandemonium that had defined me from childhood through my twenties was replaced by the steady rhythm of stability. My husband and I had carved out a life that was solid and secure. It was a stark contrast to the turbulence that once comforted me. It was a better place for me, and one I knew I needed, but that didn't mean it was easy to accept. Change, even when it was good, was unsettling. It forced me to confront what I left behind and what lay ahead.

My husband and I moved to a new place together. I was no longer afraid of the bills that would come. We built our life together with the grounding force for recovery. We were both working a program, which meant we could keep propelling forward.

By the time I turned thirty-five, I was in the place I had envisioned for this chapter of my life. My life began to stabilize. I was married, settled, and finally free from the chaos of my younger years. I quit drinking, smoking, and going to yoga and counseling. The natural process of creating life wasn't yielding the result I desperately hoped for. The pre-programmed belief that I'm 'supposed' to have children after getting married bubbled to the surface.

After we married, Scott wanted to wait a year before we started trying. I wasn't clear on why, but I respected his wishes. We decided together that our focus was child making. Scott was excited, but I was scared shitless. Was I being selfish or selfless with this request? Was I going to make a good mother? My day-to-day was better, and I knew that I was becoming who I was always supposed to be, but it didn't make the road any easier. The storm clouds that had hovered over me for years began to part, and the idea of living felt more tangible than the specter of death.

I wanted to create life. I wanted to give my child the kind of existence I had only dreamt of. Scott and I talked about having a child often in quiet, intimate conversations where hope lingered in the air, the faint glow of candlelight. During three years of trying to bring life into the world, we explored each other in ways that felt deliberate and optimistic. Each month that passed without a positive result was a bitter loss, and our dream was slipping further out of reach.

After years of living without a desire to have children, after employing the pill, an IUD, and the morning-after pill twice, I was now ready. It was almost as if I was being punished for neglecting an essential quality that the Mormon faith found the most adorning. It was another hardship that cracked my security and created doubt about the progress I'd made. After I had trouble getting pregnant, I went to specialists and began fertility treatments. My husband, ever pragmatic, had already made his peace with it, but I couldn't let go of my longing to have a child. It clung to me and left a quiet ache that gently whispered in the still of the night.

Regardless of my will to keep forging forward toward motherhood, I was always on the verge of tears in therapy. I didn't like being afraid and vulnerable all the time. I needed to stop waiting for life to happen because it was already taking place. It was passing me by quickly, and I was stuck.

Scott and I had built a good life together. It was filled with love and laughter in the moments when the weight of infertility didn't loom large. Those moments were fewer than I wanted to admit. Infertility wasn't just a challenge; it was an all-consuming force that swallowed me whole. We decided to cling to the hope that science might succeed where nature failed and try IUI treatments. Ever the dreamer, I began spinning a vivid picture of two little spirits; two sons who would one day call me "Mom." I could almost hear their laughter and see their tiny hands reaching out for mine.

That future never materialized. Each failed cycle felt like a dagger, twisting deeper into a wound that never healed. I was angry, blindingly and irrationally angry. The rage burned hot, constant, and consumed my thoughts for years. I wasn't just grieving the absence of children; I was furious at the universe for robbing me of what I believed was my destiny. I was supposed to have two sons. That belief sat heavy in my chest, unshakable and cruel.

To make it worse, my body betrayed me. I gained weight and my stomach rounded in a way that mimicked pregnancy. Acquaintances, coworkers, even strangers, would glance at me, their eyes lingering just a moment too long before asking the question I dreaded: "Are you pregnant?" Each time, the words slapped me and tore through the fragile walls I'd built to protect myself. At that time, I weighed the heaviest in my life. I knew, could even feel, people wrestling with whether they should ask. Don't ever ask. It's a question that rips at the core of a woman's self-esteem. Each time someone asked, my heart broke a little more.

Envy was the ugliest part, and I hated myself for having this emotion. My heart twisted when I saw pregnant women or heard stories about newborns. If I couldn't have children, why should anyone else? The envy poisoned my relationships and turned innocent childbirth joy into a bitter reminder of my own loss. I couldn't be around people with kids; their happiness shone a spotlight on my pain. Being at work became unbearable when several women were pregnant in my office. Their growing bellies were everywhere; it was a cruel taunt from the universe. With each failed IUI attempt, I would drive into work literally screaming out my anger before I walked through the office door.

I tried everything to make peace with my circumstances. I tried therapy, prayer, and even a psychic, who told me I needed to create dream boards and talk to my future children. "You're in limbo," she said, "disconnected from the spirits of your babies." For two weeks, I followed her advice. I closed my eyes at night and imagined their faces. I whispered to them, willing them into existence.

Each month, when my period was late by even a day, my heart leapt with cautious optimism. But hope is a cruel companion when it ends in despair. The sight of blood on the toilet paper in my workplace restroom crushed my spirit. As if my sensitivities transpired to a barren womb that had no room for anything more. I would sit there emotionally flogging myself for imagining the possibilities I failed to bring into my life.

I couldn't escape the disappointment. I'd rush to the bathroom with anxiety clawing at my throat even as I braced myself for disappointment. If my cycle had started, my panic would rise and threaten to overwhelm me. To cope, I'd leave the office under the guise of running an errand and walk to the store to escape the suffocating walls. When I returned, I'd force a smile and pretend I wasn't coming apart at the seams.

The scene was no less brutal at home. Each time I reached for a pregnancy test, hope would flutter in my chest like a desperate and fragile trapped bird. The ritual became its own form of torment: rip open the foil packet with trembling hands, shallow breath, and wait for the result. I'd set the test on the counter, pace the bathroom as if moving might speed up time, and steal glances at the strip as though it held the power to change my fate.

When the stark and unrelenting NOT Pregnant message appeared, the final, damning verdict caused my knees to buckle. I'd collapse onto the edge of the toilet seat, clutch the test in my shaking hands as if sheer willpower could rewrite the outcome. My chest tightened and my shoulders hunched under the weight of disappointment that crashed down on me in waves so intense I could barely breathe. Sobs would claw their way up my throat, raw and ugly, but I would bite them back by pressing a hand over my mouth to muffle the sound. The silence of the empty bathroom mocked me; its cold tiles and sterile fixtures bore witness to my despair.

I'd sit there for what felt like hours. The walls would close in, and their stillness amplified the panic in my mind. My reflection in the bathroom mirror was unrecognizable. I had puffy eyes with tear-streaked cheeks and a hollow expression that said I was losing pieces of myself with every failed attempt. I'd sit in the bathroom, staring at the NOT PREGNANT message, heaving with suffocating sobs.

It wasn't fair. Nothing about infertility was fair. It was a thief, robbing me of joy, replacing it with a hollow ache that lived just beneath my ribs. Watching my coworkers' bellies swell while I clung desperately to hope was an endless, torturous rollercoaster. The highs of possibility were fleeting, cruel sparks that left me bracing for the inevitable crash. The lows were cavernous envelopes that swallowed me whole with depths becoming darker with every failed attempt. Each loop of this relentless ride left me more fractured and more exhausted. Infertility doesn't care about fairness. It demands your hope and feeds on it like a parasite, only to punish you later for daring to believe.

One day, as I walked into the office breakroom, I saw it again: the ultrasound photo pinned to the bulletin board. A coworker's Christmas announcement was still posted in May. The tiny, grainy image seemed to mock me with joy and happiness I couldn't share. I stood there for a moment, breathing shallow breaths through a tightening chest. Then, without hesitation, I reached up and took it down. I told myself it didn't belong there anymore, but deep inside I knew it wasn't about the calendar. It was about me. That picture had taunted me long enough.

I tried to bury the emotions by stuffing them inside the way I stuffed food into my mouth. I used cookies, chips, fast food, anything that dulled the sharp edge of my despair. I avoided mirrors because I didn't recognize the person staring back. My weight gain had crept up slowly, but now that I was at my heaviest, I could ignore it any longer. The perky, confident girl I used to be was gone and buried beneath thick layers of grief and self-loathing. Admitting that I felt that was admitting defeat. I hid behind excuses and distractions, spent more time with family, skipped gym workouts, and neglected myself.

The stress of it all seeped into my marriage and

brought a slow, corrosive drip that eroded our foundation. Desperate to find someone to blame besides myself, I lashed out at Scott. Everything became a target, including our finances and our home. "This wasn't supposed to be my life," I told him one night, my voice shaking with anger and tears. "It's your fault." The words felt hollow even as I said them, because deep down, I knew the truth: it wasn't anyone's fault. The grief of that realization was almost too much to bear.

Month after month, I rode the emotional pendulum: elation when I thought that maybe this time would be different, and soul-crushing despair when my cycle returned to dash every fragile hope. Some weeks, the weight of it all pulled me so low I could barely function. I thought about ending it. I thought about silencing the endless loop of pain that played in my mind. I imagined the relief of turning my internal chaos into something physical, a sharp pain I could control, but even in my darkest moments, I couldn't do it. I couldn't leave Scott to carry the burden alone.

I sat one night in the quiet of our trailer and watched the dim light cast long shadows across the room. My heart was heavy, and a small voice inside me whispered that I couldn't go on like this. If I couldn't have a child, I had to find another way to move forward. I had to get healthy, not for a baby, but for myself. The thought was terrifying and liberating all at once.

Slowly, I shifted my focus. I began researching ways to break my addiction to food and healthier ways to cope with the debilitating grief. I even let myself think about adoption. The idea unfurled tentatively in my mind, a fragile bud blooming in spring. It wasn't the life I had planned, but maybe, just maybe, it could still be a life worth living.

As I stared out the window that night, listening to the rain tap softly against the glass, I felt a glimmer of something I hadn't felt in a long time: hope. It was small, almost imperceptible, but it was there. And for the first time, I let myself believe that even if I couldn't control the journey, I might still find a way to heal.

Branching Out

As 2019 began, I took my first steps to stretch outside my professional comfort zone. I began my private practice while maintaining a demanding schedule at the local hospital. I worked four ten-hour shifts. On my one free weekday, I dedicated ten hours to building my own private practice as a solo therapist. As many new therapists, I started small by renting space in another therapist's office and seeing clients who paid privately. For a mere one hundred dollars a month, I secured an office address which allowed me to credential with insurance companies and establish a legitimate presence in the field.

At first, I wanted to test the waters while maintaining the stability of my hospital job. As time went on, I found myself more drawn to the independence that private practice provides. I was no longer bound by institutional red tape or weighed down by bureaucratic inefficiencies that often valued policies over people. Instead, I could provide care on my own terms, guided by my own expertise and values rather than administrative mandates.

Stepping away from the structured environment of an established organization and into the uncertain world of entrepreneurship was a challenge. It forced me to handle everything from scheduling and billing to client retention and business development. With each step, I gained confidence in navigating the complexities of running a practice.

Eventually, the pull of autonomy became stronger than the security of employment and I decided to leave the hospital behind, committing fully to building an agency of my own.

By January 2020, my business had taken on a new level of legitimacy and complexity. I had successfully completed the credentialing process for my own behavioral health agency and navigated the extensive paperwork, policies and procedures necessary to meet state licensing requirements. The Department of Health conducted its audit and inspected everything from compliance directives to facility readiness. The initial space I rented was not ADA compliant, and I moved across the street to a new building. This was my first experience managing the many challenges of running a healthcare business. Navigating unexpected hurdles, bureaucratic demands, and identifying the need to pivot quickly to keep moving forward.

With my doors officially open, I hired a nurse practitioner and part-time master-level clinicians to support my growing contract. Transitioning from solo practice to running an agency meant stepping into an entirely new role as a supervisor. I had to shift my perspective from clinician to supervisor to administrator. The same paperwork that once frustrated me as a counselor now carried new weight, and I wasn't solely responsible for just my own notes anymore.

As agency owner, incomplete documentation meant possible penalties from the Department of Health, as well as not getting paid. I developed a newfound empathy for the clinicians, who struggled to keep up with their notes. I knew firsthand how tedious documenting services could be; however, I also understood that my business couldn't function without them.

Financial management was another steep learning curve I had to master. I had no experience handling business finances, and I outsourced managing the books to a trusted friend who I knew from recovery meetings. She reviewed quarterly reports with me, but the numbers were a foreign language. I depended on her to make sense of my business' financial health and trusted her insights as I slowly began to grasp the importance of budgeting, expenses, and cash flow.

Every day brought a mix of successes and setbacks. When I had enough staff to cover the workload, things ran well, but the days were difficult when someone called out, was let go, client needs exceeded capacity, or administrative tasks piled up. I wore every hat imaginable just to make it through. I was on the road constantly, driving throughout

Snohomish County keeping up with client care while documentation fell behind. Since I hated driving and needed every spare moment to catch up on paperwork, I hired a previous sponsee to drive me between clients. It was a win-win: she needed the extra income, and I desperately needed the time to focus. Later, when my office workload became overwhelming, I brought her on full-time to help manage operations. She turned out to be a lifesaver. She managed the administrative details, which allowed me to refocus on the bigger picture of building the agency.

I was still experiencing small bouts of panic attacks and anxiety but had resisted the pharmaceutical routine. Maybe it was pride. Perhaps it was fear of dependence, but I had convinced myself that needing medication meant I wasn't strong enough on my own. Self-love wasn't just indulgent spa days or quiet moments of reflection. It was taking my medication, allowing myself grace, and accepting help when needed.

Still, the fears lingered. The thought of losing Scott due to ailing health gnawed at me. It was an undercurrent of anxiety I couldn't silence. No matter how much I tried to focus on my progress, fear was always humming in the background, threatening to pull me back into old patterns of doubt and insecurity. My sober support program became my anchor, grounding me in honesty, open-mindedness and giving me the courage to change.

"Progress, not perfection" became my mantra. It was a daily reminder that healing wasn't about getting everything right. It was about showing up for myself, however imperfectly, day after day.

Even with support, I still struggled. I fixated on things; my mind looped around anxieties and what-ifs. I had always found comfort in solitude and retreated into my home. Deep down though, I knew that too much isolation was unhealthy.

With the COVID shutdown in March of 2020, I discovered the balance that created my mental stability. I loved staying at home. In many ways, my mild agoraphobia made teletherapy a dream. I could see clients through a screen without leaving the safety of my space. It was my time of healing. Where the world slowed down to a pace that was bearable, I thrived. The slower pace relieved my body from high anxiety and cortisol overload. I was finally able to breathe. The lockdown provided me a safe space, and I didn't feel guilty for being a homebody. I loved staying home with Scott and the puppy. I no longer took benzos consistently, and my anxiety dissipated.

Despite the internal battles, I was beginning to heal. The grief of infertility, which had weighed on me for so long, was finally feeling less suffocating. I permitted myself to sit with my emotions and be introspective without drowning in them. In an increasingly uncertain world, something beautiful happened: I found a deeper connection with my family.

For the first time in years, my childhood family came together as we never had before. We leaned on each other and offered each other support in natural and necessary ways. We started a weekly Zoom call, which was something small but incredibly meaningful. My sisters and I created a text thread where we checked in, shared our thoughts, and reminded each other that we weren't alone. Those small acts of connection became lifelines that held us together during uncertain times.

Through it all, I learned to trust myself and listen to my intuition instead of my fear. The journey wasn't linear, and it certainly wasn't easy. I was growing, piece by piece, and learning that true healing wasn't about eliminating struggle. It was about finding the strength to move through it, one day at a time.

As the business grew, so did its operational demands. I updated the equipment to meet the increasing caseload and technological needs. Then, on January 6, 2021, the insurrection at the Capitol unfolded. I remember going home early that day, overwhelmed with emotion, and watching the chaos unfold. My sisters and I were texting back and forth, trying to make sense of what was happening. It was a stark reminder that no matter how much I had on my plate, the world outside my business shifted unpredictably.

Scott's mom was confined to a nursing home and suffering from dementia, so we did window visits and a drive-by Mother's Day parade with balloons streaming from our car windows. Because of her dementia, she no longer recognized me, but she was happy to have people stop by. We had the opportunity to say goodbye to her in person dressed in gowns and masks when she passed later in 2021 in the nursing facility.

***

On the professional side, I was still learning some hard lessons about profitability. I took on an intern, then realized I couldn't bill Medicaid for their work, meaning I was donating my time without receiving reimbursement. I also lost money by bringing in a nurse practitioner primarily to give injections, unaware that the service wouldn't generate enough revenue to justify the cost. Every misstep was a learning experience that forced me to refine my business strategies and make more informed decisions.

Despite the challenges, I was evolving, not just as a therapist but as a business owner. The transition from clinical work to full-scale agency management was anything but smooth. I was building something more substantial, more sustainable, and I was doing it as the head of the agency.

I was in a hot yoga class after a long workday. If you have never participated in a class like this, know that you practice yoga in a heated and humid studio. The temperature is typically between 90 and 105 degrees Fahrenheit. Hot yoga classes are designed to replicate the climate of India, where yoga originated. The heat and humidity are believed to increase flexibility and detoxification. During the last few poses, my mind began to race; I contemplated whether I should go to graduate school, PhD or PsyD; adopt a baby; move to Arizona, Oregon, or California; or make some other drastic change. I was looking for something outward to make me feel better. I was in shavasana, the last yoga pose, and I heard a voice say, "It's not your time."

I left the studio thinking, "Okay, it is not my time to move, go to school, adopt a baby? Not my time now, so in a year?" The voice didn't return.

Rather than make any major life choices, I decided to continue the path I was on. I was stuck, needed guidance and turned to an intuitive life coach. Working with this coach reshaped my perspective in ways I didn't anticipate. She helped me see beyond the limitations I had unconsciously placed on myself. The limitations were rooted in old belief systems, particularly those ingrained by my Mormon upbringing. For years, I had minimized myself, staying small to fit expectations that no longer served me. Through our work together, I began to envision my higher self, the person I was meant to be, unbound by fear or obligation.

Spiritual growth became exponential. For the first time, I embraced the idea that I could dream big, have more, be more, and do more without feeling guilty. My coach acted as a guide. This wasn't about conforming to an external doctrine; it was about aligning with my true purpose. I had always felt a deep need to serve people, but now, that service came from a place of strength rather than sacrifice. My life was turning upside down in the best possible way.

With growth, however, came difficult realizations. One of the hardest lessons I had to learn was that my codependence was still showing up in ways that held me back. This was particularly true in my role as an employer. I had hired a friend to work for me, and instead of holding her accountable for the job she was being paid to do, I made excuses for her.

At one point, I wanted Scott to manage all the finances. He enrolled in school for two quarters and then discovered it wasn't something he had an interest in. It took me years to accept him for who he is and who he wants to be. I was disappointed, and I appreciated his honesty. I had to be vigilant in making the business work for me.

I had been in a similar place once, which made it hard for me to separate empathy from responsibility. My life coach helped me see that while compassion was important, it couldn't come at the expense of my business. It took me months to accept that my friend wasn't a good fit. I couldn't rely on her; reliability was crucial for a growing business. My intuitive life coach reminded me that the people I hired should share my vision. Otherwise, they would only hold me back. My bleeding heart made it hard to let her go. At that moment, I cared more about her well-being than I did about the survival of my company. Letting people go was painful and necessary.

Business, at its core, is about growth. If employees weren't aligned with growth, then they unintentionally hindered progress. It wasn't just that my business was evolving. My personal relationships were also shifting. As I set new boundaries and prioritized myself, the dynamic in my marriage began to change. I was making more space for myself, which my husband found irritating. He had grown accustomed to the status quo, and my newfound independence disrupted that balance. It was a challenging and essential transition that forced us to reassess our roles in the relationship.

The shifts in my personal growth also cost me two friendships. The fallout was painful, though it solidified my growth. I was no longer the person who would bend over backward to avoid conflict and sacrifice my own success for the comfort of others. When my bookkeeper told me I was becoming "too businesslike," I took it as a compliment.

"I'm not running a charity," I told her, standing firmly in my truth. "I need money to come in so I can help others and our community."

The puzzle pieces were finally coming together. My codependency had stalled my growth for years, but I was no longer that person. Losing those friendships was difficult; however, they were remnants of an old version of me. It was the version I had outgrown. As painful as that realization was, it was also freeing. I was moving forward, no longer held back by outdated beliefs, toxic patterns, or people who didn't value my vision.

Creating Peace

After years of struggling with religious trauma and its lasting impact, I have been able to set firm boundaries in my professional and personal life. Regarding spirituality and religion, I believe that we all innately want to be good human beings. To one extent or another, we find ways to tap into the energy surrounding us and balance our care for ourselves and the world around us. Some find their discipline heightened by conforming to a religious deity, while others are enlightened through other spiritual means. Whatever you call it, it is all the same. We all want acceptance and to belong.

A pivotal conversation I had with my mother on my birthday opened the door to a long-overdue discussion about the realities of my childhood. Though hesitant at first, my mother acknowledged my struggles with depression, anxiety, and religious dogma. I could tell my mom didn't really want to talk to me for very long. I leveraged the conversation to discuss everything I dealt with growing up and as an adult.

"Crystal, you know you don't have to say all the negative stuff that's happened." my mother offered.

"No, not everything in my life was negative, right?" I contemplated out loud. I was trying to gain clarity and perspective on her thoughts about my childhood. I understood that many of the things I wanted to discuss would sound accusatory, and I wanted to tread in a way that allowed my truth without disparaging my mother and her plight.

"Yes, you enjoyed camping a lot," my mother shared with optimism. "I did. I'm not bashing you, Dad, or the church. I am talking about the facts. This happened to me, and I think sharing my story could help somebody else," I responded.

I was referring to my idea of writing a book and creating a brand for myself as a religious trauma therapist. It was a bit much for my mom to understand why I wanted to disclose my experiences publicly. We ended our conversation amicably, and I thought we handled the conversation well. She called me again later that week, which was unusual for her. We have never talked twice in one week. I knew something was up, and I allowed her time to tell me what the call was about. She wanted to address the conversation we had earlier that week. "In your junior year, you were really depressed. I did try to get you into counseling. I was so worried about you."

Bringing up my dropping out of school was a sore spot, but my mother assured me that I hadn't dropped out; she had withdrawn me. I didn't see the difference between the two. She withdrew me from one school and applied for my enrollment at Windfern, an alternative high school. I loved it there. Students could walk off campus without penalty. I would go across the street, smoke a cigarette, and return more relaxed and ready for class. Windfern also had no extracurricular activities, unlike traditional high schools, which had clubs and sports.

I discussed my issues with religion, purity, and a culture that says a woman must remain a virgin and then become a porn star for her husband after marriage. I told my mom that it is very hard for a woman to switch her mentality like that. I said that I believe one reason Mormons have the highest percentage of porn consumption is because of repressed sexuality, and we need more open conversations about healthy sexual relationships.

"That's a good point," my mother said. "We're encouraging women to work outside the home. We've done studies, and children are okay if women are working outside."

The slight shifts the Mormon Church made throughout the decades, encouraging women to work outside the home, felt more like a carefully crafted public relations move than actual progress. It didn't erase the years of messages drilled into me about obedience, purity, and submission to the patriarch. The weight of those teachings still sat heavy in my chest, a stone pressing against my ribs. Even now, when I hear specific phrases, my body tenses before my mind reminds me I am free now. For me, Mormonism resembles a cult rather than an organized religion.

I knew I had to share my story with others who still felt trapped, questioning, or afraid to take the first step toward reclaiming their lives. As a therapist, I sat across from people with trembling hands and tear-streaked faces, their voices catching as they confessed how hard it is to undo faith programming. I see how guilt still lingers like a ghost even when they no longer believe. I see my younger self in them; I see the girl who spent years trying to be everything she was told she should be, only to realize that image was not her.

Of course, my life wasn't all bad. There've been moments of warmth, laughter around a campfire, and sunlit hikes where I felt that I belonged in the world as I was. I don't want to overshadow those memories, but healing from religious trauma isn't about pretending the past was better than it was. It's about honoring the truth, facing the wounds, and finally allowing myself to step into the light on my own terms.

"Mom, I really appreciate that you and I are able to talk about this." "You did the best you could, and Jesus will forgive you, and God will forgive you," she added at the end, as if it was some solace.

My path had been illuminated before me, not by doctrine or dogma, but by the quiet certainty that I was meant to share my struggles. I had spent so much of my life searching for answers in sacred texts, in the voices of religious leaders, in the rigid expectations of faith. The more I sought, the more I realized that true spiritual growth isn't about finding a single, absolute truth; it's about unlearning the fears and limitations ingrained in me.

It's been a long time since I last opened the Book of Mormon, and I feel no urgency to return to it. I am no longer searching for validation in organized religion, nor am I seeking a guru to hand me the keys to enlightenment.

Instead, I embrace a more fluid spirituality that allows me to explore and question rather than obey and conform.

I listen to a handful of spiritual teachers, yet I do not follow blindly. I take in their words, sift through their lessons, and hold on to what resonates with me and discard what does not. There is no longer an external authority dictating my beliefs. There is no voice telling me what is right or what is wrong for my soul. Instead, I am learning to trust myself, to listen to my intuition, to sit in stillness, and to recognize that I already carry the wisdom I once sought outside of myself. It's already in me. It's an ongoing process that requires patience and self-compassion. It is mine, and that is enough.

Since I first entertained the idea of writing this book, life had other plans that would stretch me in ways I never anticipated. My husband and I found ourselves stepping into the role of primary caregivers, not by design, but by necessity. When we took in our grandson, I felt a deep, unshakable pull in my heart. I longed for tiny feet pattering across the floor, the scent of baby lotion lingering in the air, and the gentle weight of a little body nestled against mine. And now, here he was, small, innocent, and full of possibility.

Joy is never untouched by sorrow, however. His mother, my stepdaughter, struggles with addiction and was unable to be fully present in his life. She had visitations and moments where she could step in or step out of his world; however, consistency was a dream still out of reach. We wanted to give her every opportunity to find her way back, to fight for her sobriety, and to heal in her own time. In the meantime, Scott and I were prepared to carry whatever weight was necessary; we love this child as primary caregivers and hold space indefinitely for his mother's return to live with him.

Seven weeks into caring for the baby, Scott and I settled into a rhythm. We had an unspoken understanding to support each other. Scott, always a night owl, had effortlessly taken the night shift. He was up until three or four in the morning anyway, long before we had this little bundle of joy in our lives. Now, those late-night hours were filled with whispered lullabies and gentle rocking in the dim glow of the living room lamp. By dawn, he would wake me with a soft nudge, our grandson cradled in his arms, ready to be passed into my care.

Days revolved around feedings, diaper changes, and the soothing repetition of lullabies hummed absentmindedly while rocking back and forth. I'd press my cheek against his soft head, breathe in that sweet scent, and feel the rise and fall of his tiny chest against mine. Some days, I would drop him off at daycare and catch up on the ever-growing list of things I had neglected at work. Most days he was with me, with his wide, curious eyes tracking my every move, and his tiny fingers wrapped around mine as if I was his anchor in this world.

The weight of his care is a blessing. I finally tempered my energy to begin to attract the things I desired most in my life. The exhaustion was deep and bone-aching, and it was nothing compared to the gratitude I feel for the chance to be here to give him stability when his world was anything but.

Still, I couldn't help but think about the impossible standards placed upon mothers, especially mothers of the Mormon faith. The expectation is that a woman should manage everything flawlessly, raise multiple children, maintain a pristine home, serve her husband's needs, and somehow never falter. It was unattainable. As I reveled in

Scott's unwavering support, I wondered how single mothers did it. How did they carry this weight alone?

One night, as Scott and I sat at the kitchen table in the quiet aftermath of another long day, he chuckled and shook his head. "You know, we need a swing shift chef in here every now and then. Someone to step in, take a shift, give us a breather."

I laughed at the truth in his words. Raising a child was not a one-person job, yet many women were expected to do it all. No wonder anxiety was rampant; no wonder burnout was the unspoken epidemic of motherhood. Yet, as I watched our grandson sleep peacefully in his bassinet with his little hand curled into a tiny fist, I knew we would do whatever it took. Because love, true unconditional love, means showing up, even when it's hard. My heart goes out to those who don't have the resources and somehow make it work though they are full of anxiety.

I also have the joy of being a grandparent to a thirteen-year-old girl. We get to spoil her and buy her whatever she wants. That is something that we could not do if we were her primary caregivers. These are the things that make my life so much fuller. The more unconditional love I give, the more I receive.

Since completing my manuscript, I began to look for podcasts and other ways to broadcast my upcoming memoir. I posted about my upcoming talk about religious trauma in November of 2024. My brother listened to my first podcast sometime during the New Year. He came at me pretty hard about my presentation. His statements were belittling, and he stated that I was emotionally immature. He kept pushing his ideas on me, which was irritating. It took me back to adolescence when I found a speck of love in my life, and my brother lashed out. It caused me to digress. I just let him know not to text me about it anymore. You simply can't engage with a narcissist.

In proper form to our family dynamic, my sister texted me a few days after our encounter with my brother. He wouldn't stop saying mean things like, "It doesn't look like you've done therapy except for maybe getting a massage." Considering all the time, effort, money, and pressure I put on myself to reach a healthier mental space, here was my brother busily protecting the Mormon Church rather than supporting his sister on her healing journey.

It eventually turned into a family group text where I stated I was stepping back from my relationship with my brother and wanted limited contact with the family about it and no engagement with my brother's negativity. Once again, my parents failed to do or say anything about his behavior. Days later, my dad sent us both a text message that said, "We love you both." It wasn't enough; I needed their support. I set a boundary and declared it to the entire family.

Religious trauma is real. It's not just a fleeting discomfort or a grudge against organized faith. It's deep, complex, and often interwoven with a person's sense of identity. For many, religious trauma stems from growing up in environments where faith was used as a weapon instead of a source of love and guidance. Trauma happens when strict doctrines instill fear, shame, and guilt to the point that they shape a person's self-worth and their ability to function in the world.

I placed the blame on the Mormon Church and the resounding nuances on the responsibility of women. It was 'normal,' and anything outside of it was openly shunned.

When I was younger, I didn't educate myself, and I continued to deal with life in the best way I knew how: by dismissing it altogether. Today, I struggle to understand why those requirements bothered me; now, I have a deeper understanding and appreciation for my past. I know, however, that without those valleys, I wouldn't be the person I am today, redefining family after ingrained doctrine. I have redefined family for myself:

- Scott is not the "head" or the "patriarch" of the family.
- We are a family, though I bore no children.
- Family is more than the traditional nuclear family.
- We share chores; there are no gender-based chores.
- We split the bills in half.

In my case, my trauma was intensified by how my family embraced religious confines that weren't just restrictive but were detrimental to my mental and emotional well-being. The pressure to conform, to be "good" by someone else's definition, and to suppress my true self for fear of judgment took a toll.

When a child is raised in a system that says your natural thoughts, desires, and even questions are sinful, the trauma doesn't just go away when they leave the faith. Trauma lingers. It burrows deep, shaping your view of yourself, your interactions with others, and how you process success, love, and happiness.

When I'm online and a stranger questions me about my religious trauma, when they write "hope I'm not traumatized on Judgment Day," I don't flinch. I stand ten toes down on what I believe because I've heard worse from my own family. My skin is thick. I've had to build that resilience to survive. What people fail to understand is that for those of us who have lived through religious trauma, leaving is not just about rejecting beliefs; it's about reclaiming ourselves.

The healthier I become mentally, the more empowered I feel. I've learned that healing isn't about getting everything right or pretending the past didn't happen. It's about radical honesty. It's about sitting with the pain, acknowledging its impact, and choosing not to let it define me anymore. The more I work on my mental health, the more I forgive myself. I forgive myself, not for anything I've done "wrong," but for all the years I spent believing I wasn't worthy.

For those suffering from religious trauma and struggling with mental health, the path forward is hard and possible. Here are eight ways to create a more fulfilling future:

1. **Acknowledge the Trauma** - Healing starts with recognition of the trauma. It's okay to admit that your religious upbringing harmed you. Your experiences are valid.

2. **Deconstruct Harmful Beliefs** - Questioning long-held beliefs isn't rebellion; it's self-discovery. Ask yourself: What parts of your faith were based on

fear? What beliefs resonate with your values today?

3. **Seek Therapy -** Find an individual and/or group therapy trained counselor. It might take time to find the "right" fit.

4. **Find Support Groups** - Peer led support groups are online or in-person for mental health, substance use disorders, and behavioral addictions. National Alliance on Mental Illness (NAMI) support groups are highly recommended.

5. **Develop Self-Compassion -** Shame and guilt don't serve you anymore. Give yourself the same grace you would offer to a friend.

6. **Set Boundaries -** It's okay to distance yourself from family members or communities that continue to harm you. Protecting your peace is not selfish; it's necessary.

7. **Reclaim Your Identity** Who are you outside of religion? What do you love? What values do you

hold, not because you were told to, but because they genuinely align with who you are?

8. **Find Meaning on Your Own Terms** - Whether it's spirituality, secular humanism, or simply embracing the present moment, life is about finding purpose in ways that empower you. This will help to let go of beliefs that lead to shame.

I'm learning to live as my higher self. I live as someone who no longer shrinks to fit inside the walls of a doctrine that never held space for me. My life isn't about perfection but truth, growth, and living authentically. That, to me, is sacred. I'm not that voiceless girl anymore!

www.ingramcontent.com/pod-product-compliance
Lightning Source LLC
Chambersburg PA
CBHW070330130626
46556CB00007B/2788